Monsoon Traders

THE MARITIME WORLD OF THE EAST INDIA COMPANY

Monsoon Traders

THE MARITIME WORLD OF THE EAST INDIA COMPANY

H. V. BOWEN, JOHN MCALEER, ROBERT J. BLYTH

SCALA

This edition © Scala Publishers Ltd 2011
Text © National Maritime Museum 2011
All illustrations © National Maritime
Museum, Greenwich, London, unless
otherwise stated below

First published in 2011 by
Scala Publishers Ltd
Northburgh House
10 Northburgh Street
London EC1V 0AT, UK
www.scalapublishers.com

In association with the
National Maritime Museum, London
www.nmm.ac.uk

ISBN 978-1-85759-674-8 (paperback)
ISBN 978-1-85759-675-5 (hardback)

Project managed by
Oliver Craske and Zoe Charteris
Edited by Sarah Kane
Designed by Isambard Thomas
Printed in Singapore

10 9 8 7 6 5 4 3 2 1

Inside front cover (endpapers on
hardback edition): PAD1361 (see fig. 48)
p.2: JOD/4/110, detail (see fig. 22)
pp.6–7: BHC1100, detail (see fig. 58)

Acknowledgements

This book is the product of significant amounts
of collective effort and co-operation. It could
not have been written or illustrated without
the collaboration of many people. The authors
would like, in particular, to thank friends and
colleagues at the National Maritime Museum.
The Photographic Department (Josh Akin,
Brendan Hennessy, Kenny Hickey, Andrew Holt,
Tina Warner and David Westwood) produced
the high-quality images that can be seen
throughout the book. Their magnificent work
speaks for itself. Thanks also to Melanie
Oelgeschlager for sourcing the external images,
and to Brendan Hennessy, Ludivine Guignard
and Kara Green for organising and co-ordinating
the delivery of the text and images. Finally, and
especially, thanks to Rebecca Nuotio for all her
help, encouragement and patience along the way.

The staff of various libraries and archives have
been extremely helpful and accommodating.
We are particularly grateful to everyone at the
British Library and at the Caird Library,
National Maritime Museum.

Finally, we would like to thank Isambard Thomas
for his design and his maps, and the team at Scala,
especially Oliver Craske, Zoe Charteris and
Sarah Kane.

Illustrations from other sources

fig. 31: © V&A Images/Victoria and Albert
Museum, London
fig. 37: © The British Library Board (WD 961, fo 5)
fig. 44: © The British Library Board (Foster, 29)
fig. 108: © Museum of London
fig. 111: Reproduced with permission of Punch
Ltd., www.punch.co.uk

Note on the Text

The spelling of place names in English has altered
considerably over time as a result of linguistic
developments and political change. In order to
convey the historical world of the East India
Company, we have chosen to use the orthography
that was current in the early modern period.

London

Amsterdam

Lisbon

Basra

Horm

*Persian
Gulf*

Madeira

Mus

*Red
Sea*

Atlantic Ocean

Mocha

Cape Verde Islands

Aden

Socc

Malindi

Mombasa

Pemba

Comoro Islands

St Helena

*Mozambique
Channel*

MADAGASCAR

Cape of Good Hope

The maritime world
of the East India Company,
1600–1858

Peking

JAPAN

CHINA

Pacific Ocean

abian
Sea

SEE MAP 2

Ternate

THE MOLUCCAS

Amboyna

NEW GUINEA

Macassar

Banda Islands

Indian Ocean

uritius

Delhi

Lucknow

Calcutta

Cambay
Surat

Makran Coast

Diu

Bay of Bengal

INDIA

Bombay

Severndroog

Masulipatam

Goa

Coromandel Coast

Malabar Coast

Madras

Seringapatam

Pondicherry

Calicut

Negapatam

Laccadive Islands

CEYLON

Kandy

Colombo

Indian Ocean

Introduction

JOHN McALEER

Coastwise – cross-seas – round the world and back again,
Whither flaw shall fail us or the Trades drive down:
Plain-sail – storm-sail – lay your board and back again –
And all to bring a cargo up to London Town!

RUDYARD KIPLING, 'The Merchantmen', in *The Seven Seas* (1896)

Less than three years after its demise in 1858, the legacy of the East India Company was assessed by the *Illustrated London News*. The popular newspaper concluded that the Company was 'the most celebrated commercial association of ancient or modern times'. Over the course of two and a half centuries, it had 'extended its sway over the whole Mogul empire'.[1] Opinions about the Company and its impact varied. Thomas Babington Macaulay, the historian and parliamentarian, delivered his judgement in a speech to the House of Commons in 1833. He believed that 'the Company had united in itself two characters, the character of trader and the character of sovereign'. In Macaulay's view, this made it 'an anomaly'. For him, the Company was 'the strangest of all governments; but it is designed for the strangest of all Empires'.[2]

Many people in Britain lauded its successes, but others questioned the propriety of a private commercial company ruling huge swathes of territory and vast numbers of people. And its impact was felt far beyond the boundaries of the Mughal Empire in India. The goods that it traded, as well as the wealth it generated, had significant and long-lasting effects on people's lives all around the globe. Nowhere was this more apparent than in Britain itself. Commodities traded by the Company, such as tea, porcelain and a dazzling array of textiles, fundamentally altered ideas of taste and fashion for millions of British people.

Rarely does a business enterprise, for that is what the East India Company was after all, make such a profound impact on the world. And all of this trading was conducted by sea. Between 1600 and 1833, ships sailing under Company colours made about 4,600 voyages from London to Asia. It was England's, and later Britain's, single biggest commercial venture. According to Captain Robert Eastwick, a Company commander, 'no finer fleet sailed the seas than that which was directed from Leadenhall Street', the Company's headquarters in the City of London.[3] Initially a relatively small player in the Asian trading world, which was characterised by complex, long-established and highly developed commercial networks, the Company eventually came to dominate the Indian Ocean region. By the 18th century, Indian provinces populated by millions of people came under British rule by virtue of Company expansion, territorial acquisition and military conquest. At its height, the Company ruled over a fifth of humanity, generated revenues in excess of the domestic British economy at the time, and commanded a quarter of a million troops in its private armies. The history of the East India Company is one of wealth, power and the pursuit of fortune. It is also one profoundly linked to the maritime world of which it formed such a crucial part.

There were, of course, trading links between Europe and Asia long before the rise of the East India Company. When King Alfred the Great sent

Sighelm on a pilgrimage to India in AD 883, he brought back 'many strange and precious union [pearls] and costly spices'.[4] But the nature of that relationship changed for ever when the Portuguese explorer Vasco da Gama reached the spice port of Calicut, on the Malabar Coast of south-west India, in 1498. He revolutionised the way that Europeans did business with Asia by sailing there, around Africa via the Cape of Good Hope. A maritime route to the East enabled western European countries to make their own way to Asia, strike their own deals and protect their own convoys. Ships could carry larger quantities of precious spices and luxurious textiles back to Europe, fuelling increased demand. In the 16th and 17th centuries, therefore, the ancient pattern of long-distance overland trade between Asia and Europe was completely altered by maritime traffic. As a result, it expanded dramatically in scale. European demand for luxury, high-value goods such as pepper and nutmeg, silks and cottons, tea and porcelain, made Asian trade immensely profitable for those who financed the voyages. The captains and sailors who were fortunate enough to return from the long voyages could also expect to make money out of their travels. And all of this maritime trade was only possible thanks to the advances in shipbuilding and maritime navigation that took place in Europe at the same time.

The Portuguese and the Dutch led the way eastwards. Their profits eventually convinced a group of London merchants to seek a royal charter to set up their own trading company, which would tap into some of this wealth. The idea of seeking royal approval to trade with the East was not new. Henry VIII had received a petition in 1511, which emphasised the need to keep up with commercial and political rivals:

The Indies are discovered and vast treasure brought from thence every day. Let us therefore bend our endeavours thitherwards; and if the Spaniards and the Portuguese suffer us not to join with them, there will be yet region enough for all to enjoy.[5]

Harbouring similar dreams of unlimited riches, a group of men trading in the City of London approached Elizabeth I. On 31 December 1600, the queen granted a royal charter to 'The Governor and Company of Merchants of London Trading into the East Indies' to deal with Asia. By the terms of the charter, 'The Company', as it became known, was given a monopoly on all English trade east of the Cape of Good Hope. Over the next two hundred years, these men and their successors altered the course of British history, had a massive impact on the people of Asia with which they came into contact and, ultimately, changed the world for ever.

Every item traded by the East India Company, every ambassador transported, and every clerk and soldier sent from Britain to India in its service was conveyed by ship. The rapid expansion of trade with Asia was the product of the Company's maritime trading endeavours, and, allied to the parallel industrialisation of Britain, generated great wealth. It was not only money that changed hands as a result of Company shipping. The acquisition and consolidation of political power in Asia was also facilitated by it. In 1834, following the loss of its final trading monopoly, the commanders of the Company's ships petitioned the Court of Directors for compensation. Keenly aware of their vital role, they remarked on how they and their predecessors had been in the Company's service for more than two centuries. They reminded the directors that it was the ships, sailors and commanders who had been 'in a great degree instrumental in acquiring and securing the now vast territories of British India for the Company and in advancing its commercial success'.[6] The rulers of British India had only been able to dominate the land because these captains had brought them to India's shores in the first place.

This book tells the story of the maritime trading world of the East India Company. It looks at the commerce it conducted and the wealth it generated. But it also explores some of the other things created by Asian trade. People moved back and forth, forging diplomatic and political ties between Europe and Asia. European rivals fought both each other and local Asian rulers for the right to trade, extract wealth and exert control over huge regions of the continent. And, in the process, the East India Company became one of the most powerful organisations the world has ever seen.

THE COMPANY BEGINS TRADING

East India Company trade followed a pattern set out from the days of its earliest voyages. The incentives of trade and profit were balanced by the need to engage with local people, negotiate with rulers and defend any gains made. The Company's ships and sailors entered a well-developed maritime trading world, which covered the whole of the Indian Ocean and the China Seas. A complex pattern of trading relationships, some stretching back thousands of years, existed between diverse regions and their respective people. Most of the links were local, covered by short journeys, not the thousands of miles travelled by East India ships on their voyages. Commanders of early Company voyages faced the challenge not only of navigating the huge distances between Europe and Asia, but also of encountering and dealing with unfamiliar commercial and trading circumstances. Even before the arrival of European trading companies, the islands of today's Indonesia, the source of some of the most sought-after spices, attracted ships and merchants from across the region. They were the furthest point to which ships from the west and junks from the north could sail and return within a year. The Chinese came south carrying silks, textiles

and porcelain, which they hoped to exchange for pepper and other spices, perfumed woods, Indian textiles and ingredients for Chinese medicine. Europeans, and the English East India Company in particular, came late to this endeavour.

The Company's first voyage was commanded by James Lancaster (fig.1). He was one of the few Englishmen with previous experience of doing business in the East. In 1588, Lancaster was involved in repelling the Spanish Armada, which he followed by spending time trading in Asia. After the establishment of the East India Company, Lancaster became a director of the newly founded enterprise. When it came to launching the venture with a trading expedition, he was the obvious choice to command the small fleet that left London in February 1601. The *Hector*, the *Susan*, the *Ascension* and the *Red Dragon*, in which Lancaster himself sailed, carried almost 500 men. The ships were armed with over 100 cannon to protect them from preying pirates, potentially hostile local Asian traders, and their traditional European foes. The small convoy was immediately delayed by contrary winds, so that 'it was Easter-day before they arrived at Dartmouth, where they spent five or six days in taking their bread and certain other provisions appointed for them'. Eventually Lancaster's fleet made its way into the Atlantic Ocean, passing Gran Canaria. They were further becalmed in the doldrums and did not reach Table Bay, at the southern tip of Africa, until 9 September, by which time they had lost 105 men from scurvy. Lancaster's ship, however, managed to avoid too many losses due to his previous experience of long sea voyages. He had 'certain bottles of the juice of limons [*sic*], which he gave to each [sailor] as long as it would last, three spoonfuls every morning fasting, not suffering them to eat anything after it till noon'.[7] They then called at Madagascar and spent nearly three weeks in the Nicobar Islands, before eventually reaching Aceh, in Sumatra, after many months at sea (fig.2). Here, the sultan permitted them to trade without paying custom dues. But, unsurprisingly, he had no use for the woollen vests and Devon trousers brought by the English and preferred them to pay for their spices in silver. Pepper was available in neighbouring Java, and it was here that Lancaster set up a trading post at Bantam in 1602. Before he left, he was given a letter and a gift to present to Queen Elizabeth – the sort of diplomatic exchange that characterised Asian trade in the centuries that followed. On their way home, the *Red Dragon* was so badly damaged in a storm that the crew wanted to abandon her. But Lancaster refused. He ordered the *Hector* to leave him and make for home, but his order was disobeyed. These two remaining ships eventually anchored safely in the Downs, a common meeting place for ships off the east Kent coast, their holds full of pepper, cloves and nutmeg. Lancaster's voyage had succeeded. He overcame difficult sailing conditions, steered clear of jealous

fig.1
James Lancaster, **English school,** 1596
James Lancaster commanded the first English East India Company expedition to Asia. He left London with four small ships and returned with a cargo of spices two years later, in 1603. He received a knighthood in recognition of his numerous achievements on behalf of the Company.
[BHC2828]

fig. 2
Aceh, by Edward Barlow,
17th century
Aceh, located on the northern tip
of the island of Sumatra, was one
of the most important locations
in South-East Asia for Europeans
hoping to trade for spices. James
Lancaster called here, and it
continued to be an important
trading location throughout the
17th century.
[JOD/4/108]

European rivals, avoided medical disaster and mutiny among his crew, negotiated with local merchants in Asia, and dealt diplomatically with local rulers and customs. This was a pattern that would be repeated as long as the East India Company traded by sea.

Based on the experience of Lancaster and others, the London-based directors of the Company gave detailed instructions to future trading voyages. Those sent with Lawrence Femell, on the sixth voyage, illustrate the mechanics of maritime trade in this period. Femell was charged with obtaining information which would help the Company in its future trading endeavours. He was ordered to report on the character of the indigenous inhabitants that he met on his voyages, the forms of government they adhered to, and what commodities they valued. In particular, the Company sought intelligence about what 'woollens and other goods of home manufacture brought from England are most vendible'. The directors were keen to barter items rather than send out money, and they requested detailed information about 'the quality, quantity, colour and price of such goods' likely to be demanded by the locals. By the same token, detailed reports about 'the commodities of each country best suited to be sent home to England, or for trade at other places in the East' were sought, as well as information about types of currency and their relative value.[8]

Impressing local rulers was a crucial aspect of Femell's role too. Special care was to be taken to uphold 'the honour of our king and the reputation of our trafficke'. Unsigned letters from King James were prepared, to be signed and distributed to local rulers along the route. Upon his arrival at Surat on the north-west coast of India, Femell was told to enquire whether or not trade concessions had already been secured with the Great Moghul, 'always remembering the honour of our king and country, and the reputations of our negotiators in those parts'. In presenting royal letters to the emperor, Femell had to take great care that they were delivered 'with that honour which may be well fitting so great a monarch'. Furthermore, he was to offer him 'some honourable present'. For this purpose, he had been provided with 'two gold rings set with emeralds', which were 'to be disposed of as presents in such manner as may most benefit the Company'.[9]

The commander of the sixth voyage, Sir Henry Middleton, was also issued with detailed instructions about the voyage itself. He was ordered to keep a journal of 'each day's navigation and of all the circumstances that may occur'. In an effort to protect the cargo, an inventory of all stores on board was to be made before they left the Thames. The crew of each ship was to assemble in the morning and evening for prayers, and the unnecessary firing of salutes was forbidden. Blasphemy, swearing, thieving, drunkenness and other disorderly conduct was to be severely punished. No gambling was permitted, as it 'generally leads to quarrellings and murders, and is

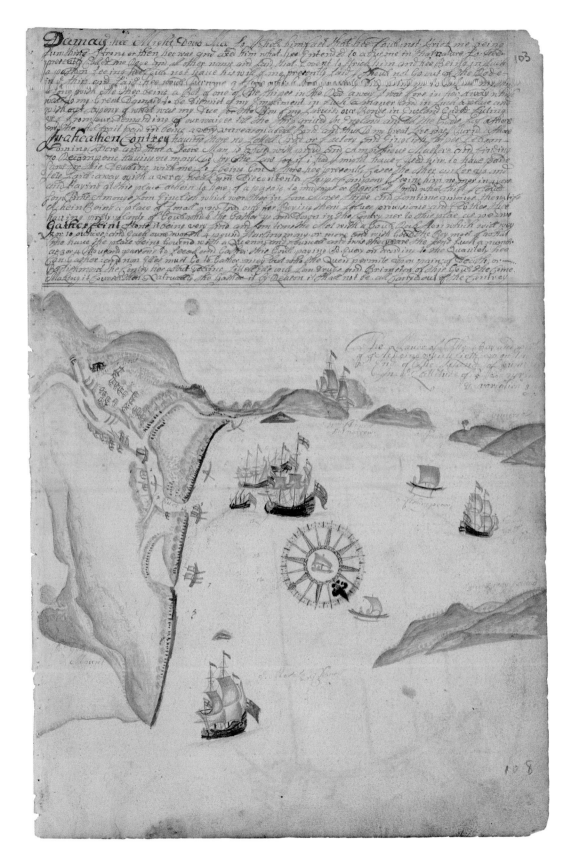

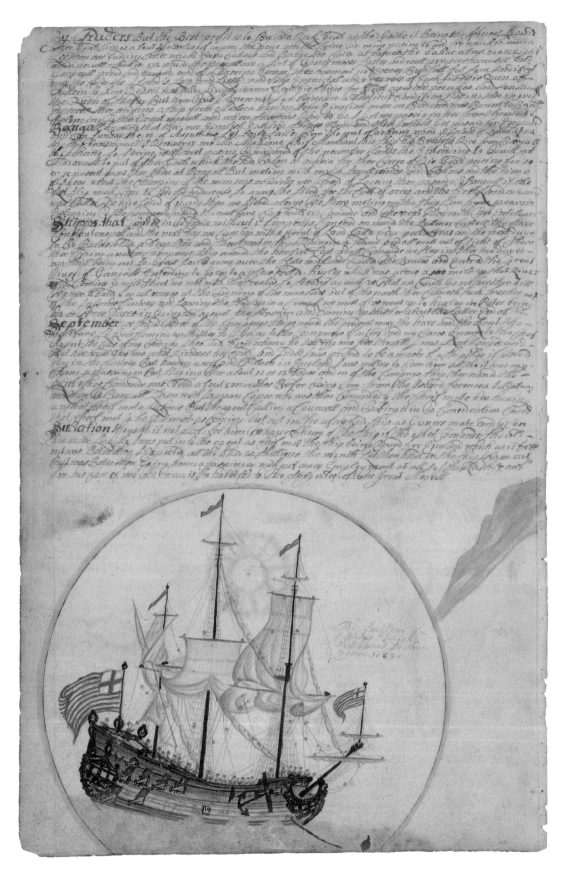

provocative of God's vengeance'. A special order was issued 'that no liquor be spilt in the ballast of the ship, nor filthiness be left within board'. Special care was to be taken to keep the ships 'sweet and clean'. The Company enjoined Middleton 'to warn the men to behave civilly and peaceably towards the natives' everywhere, 'so that supplies may be easily obtained'. With its monopoly in mind, the Company cautioned that nobody was to be allowed 'to indulge in private trade, nor to bring home more goods than will fit in a chest, the same to be registered in the purser's books'.[10] As the centuries progressed, the Company's trade with Asia became ever more extensive. But, as long as it held its monopolies, it kept tight control over who could do business, what they could trade, and with whom. Over the course of 250 years, the East India Company became the linchpin for expanding British trade and political interest in the Indian Ocean.

THE MARITIME WORLD
OF THE EAST INDIA COMPANY

The history of the East India Company reflects wider themes in British economic and political history (fig.3). Its story is also the story of remarkable individuals, like James Lancaster, who influenced the way the Company did business. The impact of technological and communication advances affected the Company too. But central to all of this was the Company's trading activities, with its insatiable drive for profits and making money. Thousands of individual voyages yielded vast profits. But, in doing business on such a scale, the Company needed to meet and engage with a variety of people. Diplomacy went hand in hand with trading. As did war and conflict – the results of defending trade and protecting profits. These latter two themes were inextricably linked to the impulses of commerce. They were both conducted in support of trade, but they were also consequences of that trade. This symbiotic relationship between trade, diplomacy and conflict runs through the entire history of the East India Company and its maritime world.

fig.3
The Ship *Delight,*
by Edward Barlow, 17th century
Ships such as this, the *Delight,* were the type of vessel used by the Company in the first century of its existence. Edward Barlow, who kept an important illustrated journal of his experiences, sailed in this ship in 1682 as the chief mate, earning £6 5s a month.
[JOD/4/108]

I

Uncertain beginnings
The East India Company, 1600–1709

H. V. Bowen

When the great political economist Adam Smith first published *The Wealth of Nations* in 1776, he made the famous and often-quoted observation that the late-15th-century European discoveries of America and the sea route to the East Indies via the Cape of Good Hope should be regarded as 'the two greatest and most important events recorded in the history of mankind'.[1] In one sense Smith was quite correct because these near-simultaneous discoveries served slowly to forge the maritime connections between Europe, the New World and Asia that led to the emergence of a transoceanic world economy defined by long-distance flows of bullion and commodities. But it should not be thought that the experience of the Europeans as 'discoverers' was in any way similar in the Atlantic and Indian Oceans. As Smith himself well knew, in the Atlantic world different European nations were able to create their own overlapping systems of trade and colonies where none had previously existed. But when they sailed into the Indian Ocean they entered a very different extended maritime space that was already defined by the existence of a series of long-standing, complex and interconnected regional maritime economies. This meant that, from the beginning, Europeans were able to develop an Atlantic trading system that was harnessed to their own needs. In the Indian Ocean, by contrast, they long remained marginal actors who were incapable of exerting much in the way of any real control or influence across the region as a whole.

THE INDIAN OCEAN TRADING WORLD

The world that Europeans entered when they first rounded the Cape was an already mature and sophisticated maritime region that had long been well attuned to moving in time with the rhythms that arose from a unique set of natural and climatic conditions. The Indian Ocean and the basin in which it sits is profoundly influenced by the fact that to the north lies the great land mass of Asia, a continent whose extensive mountain ranges give rise to the monsoon rains and winds that blow in alternating directions during different seasons of the year. On land the monsoons shaped patterns of vegetation and agriculture, while at sea the shifting winds and currents had long determined the movements of sailing vessels. Arising from these natural conditions was a world characterised by both diversity and unity. It was diverse in the sense that it incorporated an enormous range of people, traditions and cultures located on far-flung shores, from East Africa to South-East Asia; and yet it was simultaneously unified by a web of maritime linkages created by the patterns of wind and tide. This made for a cosmopolitan maritime world on the move, which enabled the circulation of ideas, cultures, religions and commodities around the ports and islands that served as the key nodal points within a series of overlapping regional economies centred on the Arabian Sea, the Bay of Bengal and the South China Sea (figs 4 and 5).

The Arabian Sea trading zone incorporated the Red Sea, Persian Gulf, much of the east coast of Africa and the west coast of India; the Bay of Bengal zone included the east coast of India, the Gangetic Delta, Burma, Malaya and the island of Sumatra; the South China Sea zone was centred on the Indonesian Archipelago and the Philippines, but also included the Chinese port city of Canton. Trade patterns were shaped primarily by the movement of goods within and around these zones, but commodities were also carried between the zones, with long-distance commerce being a feature of the Indian Ocean world long before the arrival of any Europeans. This meant that ports such as Aden, Muscat, Hormuz, Cambay, Calicut, Malacca and Canton became places that were frequented by a great number of merchants from different places. They developed into emporia where it was possible to trade in a wide range of products from across the Indian Ocean as a whole. Europeans were fascinated by this process of exchange and, although attention tended to be centred on exotic or luxury products

fig.4
Indian Ocean,
by **Battista Agnese**, 1554
Winds and currents influenced all maritime trade in the Indian Ocean. As well as depicting the eight winds, this map also shows three ships sailing on the ocean: one Portuguese and two Chinese. Enthroned rulers can be seen in the lands surrounding the ocean.

[P/24/(7)]

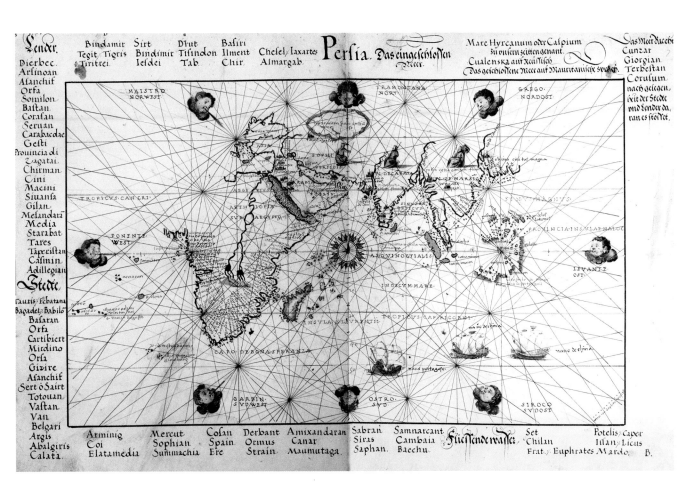

fig. 5
The Indian Ocean, from
*The Great and Newly Enlarged Sea
Atlas or Waterworld*,
by Johannes van Keulen,
published in Amsterdam, 1682
The elaborately decorated
cartouche, in the top left-hand
corner of this map, illustrates the
type of people and scenes that
European traders expected to
find on their travels in Asia.

[PBD8037]

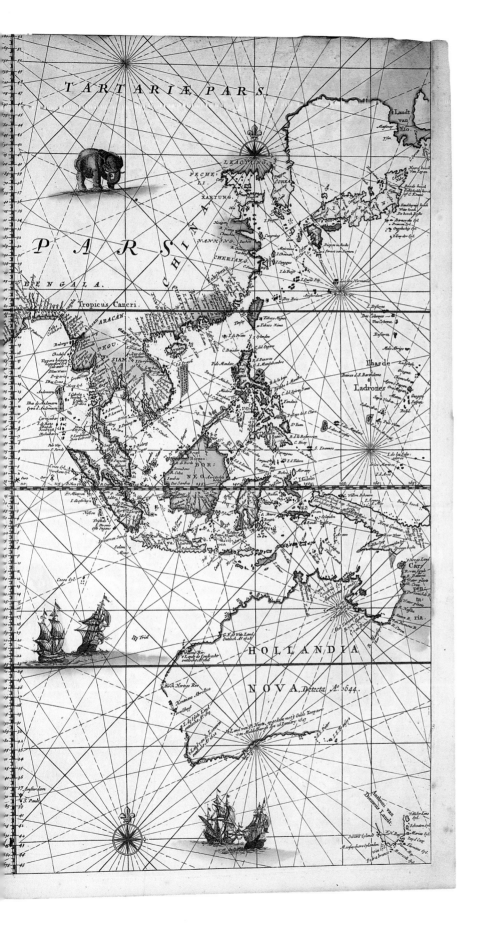

TARTARIÆ PARS

P A R S

CHINA

LEAOTUNG

PECHE-LI

XANTUNG

NANKING

CHEKIANG

BENGALA.

Tropicus Cancri.

ARACAN

PEGU

SIAM

BORNEO

NEO

Java

HOLLANDIA

NOVA Detecta Aᵒ 1644.

Ladrones

Ilhas de

Landt van Eso

COREA

to the exclusion of mundane foodstuffs and bulk commodities, writers often highlighted the ways in which the great port cities facilitated long-distance commerce across the three main trading zones. Thus when the historian David Macpherson later reflected on the Indian Ocean trade of the early 17th century, he reminded his 19th-century readers that Malacca had been at the centre of a great web of trade that extended far and wide:

There the merchants from all the more Eastern countries met with those of Hindoostan and the Western Coast of the Indian Ocean; and every one procured what was in request in exchange for what was redundant in his own country. The cities of Calicut, and Cambay on the west side of Hindoostan, Ormus in the Persian Gulf, and Aden on the South Coast of Arabia, were particularly enriched by the trade of Malacca; and they also trade to Pegu for rubies and lacker, to Bengal for cloths (now called piece goods), to Calicare (or Kilcare) for pearls, to Narsinga for diamonds, to Ceylon for cinnamon and rubies, and to the coast of Malabar for pepper, ginger, and many other kinds of spices.[2]

Contemporaries recognised that these extended connections ensured that far-distant ports became dependent upon one another, with maritime trading exchanges supplying their lifeblood. As the Portuguese apothecary Tome Pires put it in the early 16th century, 'Malacca cannot live without Cambay, nor Cambay without Malacca, if they are to be very rich and prosperous'.[3]

fig.6
Pechili trading junk, 20th century
The Chinese, travelling in ocean-going junks like this, were doing business across and around the Indian Ocean for centuries before European traders arrived in the region.

[AAE0166]

The connections between Indian Ocean ports were forged by a wide range of ocean-going vessels, some of which were capable of undertaking long-distance voyages. For example, from the 12th century onwards there is evidence of Chinese merchant activity in the western Indian Ocean, at ports in the Persian Gulf and on the Malabar Coast. During the early 15th century, a series of six maritime expeditions was dispatched from China under the overall command of Admiral Cheng Ho. The scale and range of these operations was very considerable, with the first expedition involving over 60 great treasure ships and almost 30,000 men, and some of the later voyages claimed to have reached as far as the coast of East Africa. China's intrusion into the Indian Ocean ended abruptly in 1433 when the Chinese authorities withdrew their sponsorship of long-distance trade, but Cheng Ho's expeditions highlight the sophistication of Asian shipbuilding. Junks were built to carry bulk cargoes over long distances, and continuities in design mean that Pechili trading junks of the early 20th century can be traced back to the early 15th century (fig. 6). Vessels such as these were well adapted to monsoon sailing conditions, and their effective use illustrates that long-distance trade existed long before the arrival of Europeans (fig. 7). In other words, Europeans did not create the trading world of the Indian Ocean. Instead,

fig. 7
A Trading Junk, **Chinese school, 19th century**
The stern of the junk in the painting carries an inscription invoking good fortune. The three Chinese characters, 'Li Wan Jin' (from right to left), translate literally as 'May our profit be ten thousand pieces of gold'.

[BHC1182]

they entered it as outsiders and took their place among a whole host of mariners and merchants who were there jostling for position and advantage (figs 8 and 9).

FIRST STEPS

European trade with Asia existed long before the discovery of the all-sea route to the East via the Cape. From at least Roman times there had been a steady flow of commodities into Europe along the great Silk Road and other overland routes which passed mainly through Byzantium to the eastern Mediterranean, from where substantial consignments were shipped onwards by Venetian merchants in particular. There was considerable European demand for pepper and spices such as nutmeg, cloves, cinnamon, ginger and cardamom, which had a number of culinary and medicinal uses. The presence of silks, textiles, sandalwood and porcelain ensured that the trade was always varied and high volume in content. Indeed it has been estimated that, by 1500, the pepper and spices passing through Venice amounted to well over three million pounds (lbs) a year. From Venice, Asian commodities were carried by land and sea to markets and fairs across Europe and, as far as the English were concerned, by the mid-16th century the key place of access to goods from the East was in fact very close to home in Antwerp in the Spanish Netherlands. By then, however, Antwerp was also being supplied with Eastern goods that were being shipped from Asia via the Cape by the Portuguese, who re-exported them from Lisbon.

This establishment of a bulk maritime trade by the Portuguese was a key development, for in the long run it altered the entire structure and organisation of Europe's trade with the East. Overland trade did not disappear overnight, and it remained important for some time to come. Yet attention was increasingly focused on mounting a challenge to the Portuguese. Since Vasco da Gama's arrival at Calicut in south-west India in 1498, the Portuguese had successfully captured and controlled a network of ports as they endeavoured to monopolise the trade of the Indian Ocean. This network was centred on Goa, which had been taken in 1510, and included Colombo, Diu, Hormuz and Malacca. Crucially, the Portuguese also built up a significant presence in Mozambique, which acted as a way-station for ships travelling between Lisbon and Goa. The Portuguese thus laid down a system to facilitate their own involvement in the trade in pepper and spices, but they also acted with aggressive intent by attempting to exert control over other traders through the issuing of licences or *cartazes* and the collection of taxes. Their actions marked a change in the rules of the game for those who had long traded in the Indian Ocean, but they also represented

fig. 8
Chinese Trading and Fishing Vessels,
after Thomas Daniell, 1810
[PAD0368]

fig. 9
Malaye Proas,
after Thomas Daniell, 1810
European artists and travellers, such as Thomas Daniell, recorded and remarked upon the vessels used in the region and the continued importance of maritime trading routes and connections.
[PAD0021]

a serious challenge to other European nations who wished to benefit from trade with Asia.

Although the early advances and successes of the Portuguese were widely known, it took the English some considerable time to galvanise themselves into action, largely because trade with Antwerp met much of the growing domestic demand for spices and textiles. But without any direct participation in Asian trade, England was always vulnerable to shortages or breakdowns in the supply chain, and the worst fears of ministers and merchants were realised during the third quarter of the 16th century when deteriorating relations with Spain resulted in a complete stoppage of trade at Antwerp. The political uncertainties that caused this denial of access to Eastern goods in west Europe lay behind English attempts to enter directly into the trade with Asia. Perhaps rather surprisingly, it was not the Cape sea route that captured attention in the first instance; instead, efforts were made to find a way into the overland trade with Asia. Merchants of the Muscovy Company organised a series of ambitious though unsuccessful commercial expeditions from Russia to Persia during the 1560s and 1570s. Then a group of merchants who had begun trading with Turkey formed what became known as the Levant Company. As part of this concerted effort to secure a more regular supply of Asian commodities to England, they endeavoured to establish overland links with India. The most notable manifestations of this enterprise were the commercial expeditions led by the relentlessly optimistic John Newbery, who proposed setting up a chain of English trading posts between Aleppo and India. Although these expeditions were failures in a commercial sense, they did add greatly to the fund of English knowledge about trade in Asia, especially because one of Newbery's surviving companions, Ralph Fitch, travelled far and wide before reaching Malacca. Fitch passed on much practical information to merchants in London, but he also left them in no doubt as to how difficult it would be for them to trade in places where there was already a strong and well-established Portuguese presence.

For all the interest and ambition that English merchants showed in initiating an overland trade with Asia, it was to be the successful mastery of the sea route via the Cape that would eventually enable them to gain a commercial foothold in the Indian Ocean world. The practical difficulties involved in organising and safeguarding an overland route to Asia were all too evident to those who aspired to conduct a regular and high-volume trade with the East. Yet establishing a maritime connection offered no easier alternative because it posed a number of extreme challenges to mariners and merchants. In any period, a sailing voyage from Europe to Asia tested shipbuilding, navigational and seamanship skills to the limit. But in an age before accurate maps, charts and timekeeping the risks and dangers were very considerable indeed. Moreover, Portuguese and Spanish dominance of all sea routes that passed through the South Atlantic restricted English freedom of movement, which explains why early attention had been focused on finding an alternative north-west or north-east sea passage to the Orient. The failure of these often heroic efforts meant England was left with no alternative other than to try to assert itself against its rivals, and it was encouraged in this ambition by the growing maritime strength that manifested itself in the defeat of the Spanish Armada in 1588.

It cannot be said that the growth of direct English maritime commercial links with Asia arose from any grand design or carefully formulated plan. Instead, the steps leading to the establishment of an enduring connection with the East were of an uncertain and hesitant nature, with the founding of the East India Company marking the end of a lengthy period of false starts and failure for English mariners and merchants. Indeed, while those in England were being made increasingly aware of the great commercial wealth of Asia, the focus of their attention usually lay elsewhere, and during the last quarter of the 16th century they were especially preoccupied with the general European scramble for South American riches and colonies. Hence, when contact was made with the East Indies or Spice Islands it tended to be as a by-product of other maritime enterprises, and voyages into the Indian Ocean usually formed part of broader attempts to compete with Portugal and Spain in the wider world. For example, Drake's famous circumnavigation of the world between 1577 and 1580 developed from what began as a voyage of plunder and reconnaissance of the South American coast (fig.10). Thus although he returned to England via Celebes, the Moluccas, Java and the Cape, Drake's crossing of the Indian Ocean from east to west represented a search for a safe homeward passage rather than any premeditated attempt to undertake a trading voyage to the Spice Islands.

Drake's success did excite wide interest and greatly stimulated English maritime ambition by drawing attention to the potential gains to be made in the East Indies, yet the English found it especially difficult to translate that ambition into sustained achievement in the Indian Ocean. There was often a confusion of purpose and a lack of clarity in the minds of many commanders who by instinct preferred plunder to trade, and this contributed to a series of failures. Such was the case with Edward Fenton whose ill-fated expedition of 1582–83 set out for the Moluccas but then diverted to Brazil, where it met with a succession of disasters and setbacks. Thomas Cavendish had some degree of success with his Pacific voyage of 1586, but the 1590s proved to be a dismal decade during which English attempts to establish a presence in the Indian Ocean failed miserably. The plundering voyages of Cavendish (1591), James Lancaster (1591) and Benjamin Wood (1596) all eventually resulted in the heavy loss of men, money and ships, and little was done to promote trade or commercial reconnaissance. Yet, despite these

fig.10
Medal commemorating Drake's voyage, 1577–80, c.1589
This silver medal was struck by Michael Mercator and sold in London in 1589. The dotted line indicates the route taken by Drake on his circumnavigation of the globe, and shows the ships passing the Spice Islands.

[MEC0004]

setbacks, enticing prospects of Asiatic riches continued to be dangled before English merchants, none more so than in 1587 and 1592 when the cargoes of two captured homeward-bound Portuguese carracks, *San Filippe* and *Madre de Dios*, were sold in London where they generated a great deal of public interest.

By the 1590s, the recent experiences of the English in the Indian Ocean underlined the extent to which there was a need for changes in attitude and outlook if a successful East India trade was to be built up. Searching for an overland route, or funding voyages of plunder, offered only limited prospects for long-term success, and logic was beginning to dictate that new ways had to be found of conducting, funding and organising a costly and unpredictable transoceanic maritime trade. More to the point, the Dutch were demonstrating that it was possible to offer a serious and very direct challenge to Portuguese domination of the East India trade, and they did so by using the Cape sea route. This process began in 1597 when a Dutch vessel returned from Bantam (on the western end of Java) with a cargo of pepper. During the following year, the Dutch fitted out no fewer than 22 ships for the East India trade, and in 1599 the merchants of the Levant Company were greatly alarmed by the news that six ships led by Jacob van Neck had returned to Holland laden with pepper and spices (fig.11). These successes paved the way for the eventual creation of a Dutch East India Company, and this happened in 1602 when various East Indian enterprises were merged to

fig.11
The Return to Amsterdam of the Second Expedition to the East Indies on 19 July 1599, by Andries van Eertvelt, *c.*1610
The Dutch were among the first Europeans to recognise the potential profit to be made from maritime trade with Asia. This painting shows the return to Amsterdam of ships from the second Dutch trading expedition to the East Indies in 1599, with the city visible on the right.
[BHC0748]

form the *Vereenigde Oostindische Compagnie,* or VOC (fig.12). There was no denying the threat to English merchants, but at the same time Dutch successes pointed to the growing weakness and vulnerability of the Portuguese position in the Indian Ocean, something that became all the more apparent when a translation of Jan Huyghen van Linschoten's detailed account of the East Indies was published in London in 1598. The signs were clear, and English merchants were now faced with the very real prospect of the Dutch monopolising the supply of spices to Europe. This served to concentrate minds, and leading members of the Levant Company were left in no doubt that they had to follow the Dutch example by establishing a new sea route to the East that passed around the Cape of Good Hope (fig.13).

THE CREATION OF THE ENGLISH COMPANY

It was against this background that firm plans for the establishment of an English East India Company were laid during the summer of 1599. Members of the Levant Company played a leading role in this process, gathering information (much of which was provided by Richard Hakluyt) and lobbying the Crown extensively for the right to conduct an exclusive maritime trade with the East. They made good use of their contacts at the court of Elizabeth I and were careful to set out the advantages that would accrue to the Crown as well as to the Company. In return for a monopoly of trade, the Crown could expect revenue from imported goods and the Company would take a lead in offering a direct commercial challenge to the Dutch. At the same time, the promoters of the fledgling company held meetings and opened up a subscription list. The first list of subscribers was compiled on 22 September 1599, and it contained 101 names. At its head was the Lord Mayor of London, Sir Stephen Soame, who, like many other early investors, was a member of the Levant Company. His presence illustrated the way that the nascent Company drew together many leading figures from across the overlapping financial, commercial and political worlds of the City of London. Thus in the early meetings of the Company, aldermen such as Nicholas Mosley and Richard Hallydaie rubbed shoulders with traders such as Oliver Style, a grocer, James Dean, a draper, and Henry Bridgeman, a leather seller. In all, the first subscribers contributed £30,133 to the venture, and this figure later more than doubled to the very considerable sum of £68,373. The organisational form to be taken by the Company also began to become clear, and a petition submitted to the Privy Council on 25 September 1599 asked, among other things, that a monopoly of trade be granted, together with formal incorporation, 'for that the trade of the Indias, being so farre remote from hence, cannot be traded but in a joint and unyted

fig.12
Votive model of a Dutch East Indiaman, 1657
Built at a scale of 1:33, this model represents a 240-ton ship. Models such as this were made to hang in churches, to remind the congregation of their reliance on God's favour for successful maritime endeavours. It also emphasised the perils encountered by those travelling at sea.
[SLR0365]

fig.13
Table Bay, **by Edward Barlow, 17th century**
Because of the long distances involved, ships travelling to Asia needed safe and secure places to pick up supplies and do repairs en route. Even though it was the Dutch who established a fortified station at the southern tip of Africa in 1652, it was widely used by other European trading companies.
[JOD/4/87]

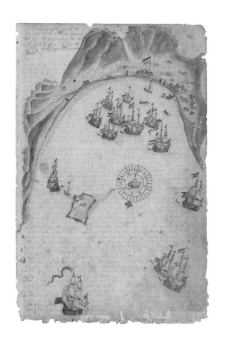

stock'.[4] From the very outset, therefore, it was envisaged that this would be a large-scale enterprise that would be armed with the authority, backing and financial resources necessary to compete with the Portuguese and, more especially, the Dutch. But in spite of widespread political and financial support, the Company experienced a lengthy birth and it was not in fact until 1600 that a royal charter was granted. On 31 December 1600, 219 adventurers were incorporated as 'The Governor and Company of Merchants of London Trading into the East Indies'. They were granted the exclusive privileges of English trade with countries beyond the Cape of Good Hope and the Straits of Magellan for 15 years. Thus came into being the commercial organisation that was later to become popularly known as the 'East India Company'.

From the very beginning, the Company acted as a joint-stock enterprise to pool the financial resources of investors, which was very necessary in view of its extremely heavy costs and overheads, as well as the need to tie up trading capital for long periods of time. This makes it tempting to see the Company that emerged in 1600 as a fully formed, modern firm but this is misleading. In terms of methods and organisation it is certainly possible to discern practices that are recognisably modern. For example, a governor and 24 annually elected 'committees', or directors, took responsibility for the Company on behalf of its investors, and a series of rules and regulations set out in some detail the duties of executive and administrative personnel. This served to bring a sense of logic, order and much-needed stability to the whole complex business of organising long-distance trading voyages, and many of the early features of the Company were indeed to survive through to the end of its days in 1858. Far less modern though were the Company's investment practices, and it took a long time for a permanent joint stock to be set up. Between 1601 and 1612, investors were obliged to subscribe funds to single voyages, and they then had to wait some considerable time before receiving any return in the form of dividend payments. In 1613, after the 12th voyage to the East Indies, fixed-term joint stocks came into being, but it was not until 1657 that the Company's finances were finally organised as a permanent joint stock, a key development that facilitated long-term investment as well as the trading of shares.

The institutional character of the East India Company was formed by its founding members and those who subsequently invested in its stock. The Company was established as a 'London' company, and it remained located in the capital throughout its long existence, which meant that it was always populated by members of the metropolitan financial, mercantile and political elite. In its early days, strong links were retained with the Levant Company, but many of its stockholders held broad portfolios of investment in overseas enterprise and were interested in the commercial expansion that was beginning to take place in the Atlantic world as well as the Indian Ocean. A good example of this type of merchant-financier is Sir Thomas Smythe, who took the lead in directing the early development of the Company. He was the first governor (or chairman) of the Company, serving again in that role between 1607 and 1610, and from 1614 until 1621. At various points, Smythe was a member of several companies, and he served as governor of the French, Levant, Muscovy, North-West Passage and Virginia Companies. This placed him at the very heart of English overseas enterprise, as a visionary who relentlessly pursued the increase of trade and commerce in all quarters. But Smythe also carved out a career for himself in the civic politics of London, serving as auditor, alderman and sheriff of the City. His great breadth of practical experience, influence and knowledge was essential for the early growth of the fledgling company. Of course, as a conspicuously successful figure Smythe was not typical of all investors, many of whom were of the passive or 'sleeping' type, but he was nonetheless representative of the type of individual who was keen to share in the commercial opportunities that could be exploited by the Company.

The original aim of the Company was to trade with the islands of the Indonesian Archipelago over which the Portuguese had no control, with a view to obtaining a regular supply of pepper and spices at source. The Dutch had already demonstrated that it was possible to trade successfully in the area, but the Company was confronted with several problems of a practical nature. For example, it proved difficult to finance the first voyage, although almost £70,000 was eventually subscribed, and it was recognised that there was only limited demand in the East for the staple English export, woollen cloth. The problem of export cargoes long affected the Company, and from the very beginning it employed the deeply controversial solution of shipping out bullion as a means of providing the purchasing power that was necessary for the procurement of large consignments of pepper and spices. Opponents of the Company used this export of precious metals as a stick with which to beat the Company because it was perceived as a drain on the country's finite supply of money. Nevertheless, the first company voyage carried out £21,742 in silver dollars and only £6,860 in goods, mainly woollen cloth, tin and lead. Also evident from the outset was an embryonic trading method that was based upon leaving agents, who were known as 'factors', in key locations so that they could procure consignment commodities for Company ships visiting in later years.

After six months of detailed planning, the Company's first voyage left London under the command of James Lancaster in February 1601. The flagship was the 600-ton *Red Dragon*, formerly the *Scourge of Malice*, which carried 38 guns and 200 men. She was accompanied by three former Levant trading vessels: the *Hector* (300 tons and 108 men), *Ascension* (260 tons and

82 men) and *Susan* (240 tons and 88 men), all of which carried 24 guns. The fifth ship in the fleet was a small victualling vessel, the *Gift*, that was set adrift once its supplies had been used. This was a powerful fleet in terms of its manpower, and the Company tried to ensure that it was in the best hands. While Lancaster was in overall command, he was accompanied by others with experience of Asian waters, including a pilot-major, John Davis, who had served as a pilot on a Dutch voyage to the East Indies. Nonetheless, the outward voyage was not without its difficulties, and heavy losses of crew members to scurvy obliged the small fleet to spend seven weeks at the Cape and over three months at Madagascar. These long delays meant that, in all, it took Lancaster 16 months to reach Aceh on the island of Sumatra. To make matters worse, the English merchants were to be disappointed with the trading conditions they found there because pepper was both scarce and expensive. Lancaster was, however, able to derive considerable commercial advantage from the plundering of a large Portuguese vessel carrying calicoes and other Indian commodities, and these captured goods greatly strengthened his ability to trade. The *Ascension* and *Susan* were sent back to England fully laden with pepper, but Lancaster sailed on with the *Red Dragon* and *Hector* to Bantam where, arriving in December 1602, trade was conducted much more easily than had hitherto been the case. In large part this was because Bantam was a flourishing port that not only exported a great amount of pepper from its hinterland but also enjoyed a brisk trade with other parts of the East Indies. This marked it out as a suitable place for the establishment of an English 'factory', and necessary permissions were

fig.14
A Dutch Settlement in India,
by Ludolf Backhuysen, *c.*1670
Many European trading powers established territorial presences in Asia in the 17th century.

[BHC1933]

obtained from the local king. As a result, when Lancaster's ships left for home the following February, carrying large quantities of pepper, three merchants and eight others were left in Bantam to look after the Company's interests, and this small and vulnerable trade delegation represented the first permanent English presence in the region.

Although Lancaster and his four ships had all returned to London safely by September 1603, the Company's first voyage was not a conspicuous success in financial terms, largely because the importation of pepper estimated to amount to over one million pounds served only to glut and dislocate the market. This was an early lesson in the need for the Company to import a variety of goods, and, in the years that followed, efforts were made to open up a wider range of trading connections, not just in the East Indies but elsewhere in the Indian Ocean and beyond. The aim was to move beyond a bilateral trade focused narrowly on the procurement of pepper towards a model that was more flexible and allowed for the purchase of a greater variety of commodities for the home market. At the same time, it had proved difficult to dispose of English goods at Bantam, and it was recognised that commodities such as cotton textiles or calicoes procured in India could be exchanged much more easily for pepper and spices. This led to the Company becoming involved in intra-Asian, or what was known as 'country', trading. Although most of the Company's early voyages still had Bantam as their ultimate destination, efforts were soon made to divert some ships elsewhere, first to the Spice Islands and then to well-established ports in the western Indian Ocean. The success of the second voyage, led by

Henry Middleton in 1604, was based upon the procurement of cloves and nutmeg in the Banda Islands and Amboina in order to supplement pepper bought at Bantam and this served only to encourage such a broadening of activity. As a result, from the third voyage of 1606 onwards Company ships were sent ever more regularly to India. Most notably, Surat on the west coast of India was visited for the first time in 1608 and a factory was set up there in 1613 (fig.14). In a parallel development, a small trading station was founded in 1611 on India's eastern Coromandel Coast at

Masulipatam in the Kingdom of Golconda. From here Company merchants were to buy calicoes for onward shipment to Indonesia. This thrusting early strategy meant that by 1614 the Company's commercial links already extended from the Red Sea to Japan, where at Hirado the Company hoped to exchange commodities for locally produced silver. Although many of these far-flung connections were short-lived they did nonetheless allow the Company's trade to become ever more integrated, with English ships increasingly carrying goods between Asian ports as well as to and from Europe.

FLUCTUATING FORTUNES

The first two decades of the East India Company's history were necessarily a time of experiment, trial and error, but in many ways these early years were successful. Trade began to be organised into a regular pattern based upon annual voyages, a network of factories was placed under the direction of a 'factor-general', William Keeling, in 1615, and investors enjoyed very good returns on their money. The 12 separate voyages between 1601 and 1612 earned an average profit of 155 per cent, with four of them each earning spectacular returns of over 200 per cent. Yet the Company remained vulnerable to a number of threats, and the 40 years or so after 1620 were characterised by uncertainty and crisis both at home and abroad.

First and foremost the Company had to assert itself against challenges that were made to its position in the East by the Portuguese and the Dutch. Successful engagements were fought against the former in the waters off Surat in 1612 and 1615, but the powerful Dutch Company proved to be a much more formidable opponent, and it endeavoured to obstruct the English at every turn. In particular, the Dutch pressurised the Company into withdrawing from the Moluccas in 1622, and this was swiftly followed by the infamous event that become known as the 'Amboina massacre' when ten English merchants were tortured and executed by the Dutch, who had accused them of plotting to seize their fort on the island. At the same time, financial retrenchment led to the abandonment of factories at Ayuthia in Siam, Patani in Malaya, and Hirado in Japan in 1623. This scaling back of operations created the impression that the Company was fast losing ground to the Dutch. In fact, withdrawal from the Moluccas did not put an end to English participation in the spice trade, but the difficulties experienced in the East Indies did briefly prompt those in London to consider suspending all commercial operations in 1627. This did not happen, but greater attention was now paid to India and indeed Persia, where three voyages were sent between 1628 and 1630.

At home the Company was also vulnerable, and during the first half of the century its domestic foundations were regularly shaken by political crises. In part this was because the Company's exclusive privileges had to be renewed on a regular basis, and on such occasions a stout defence always had to be offered against those who were excluded from the East India trade. At the same time, hard-pressed monarchs often endorsed rival East India projects as a means of raising funds, and such an attitude encouraged groups of merchants to combine in order to mount direct commercial challenges to the Company. As early as 1604, James I had backed an interloping voyage to the East Indies under the command of Sir Edward Michelborne. In 1618, he permitted the creation of a Scottish East India Company led by Sir James Cunningham. In the latter case, the threat to the Company was only averted through a combination of vigorous lobbying at Court and the payment of a £20,000 'loan' to the king. Yet more seriously, in 1637 Charles I issued a patent to Sir William Courteen whose new commercial organisation was permitted to trade in Asian waters not frequented by the East India Company. This was a further attempt by the Crown to squeeze benefit from the East India trade but, during the 15 or so years of its existence, Courteen's Association achieved little of note and perhaps most conspicuously it failed to establish a settlement on the island of Madagascar.

The floating of ventures to rival the East India Company was indicative of the fact that there was always considerable opposition to the idea that English trade with Asia should be conducted as a monopoly enterprise. In part, this opposition came from those disaffected merchants who found themselves excluded from the trade, but there was also a broad range of critics who raised philosophical and economic objections to the use of monopolies. Some regarded the use of exclusive privileges by the Crown as nothing less than an assault on the rights and freedoms of the individual, while others argued that monopolies inflicted considerable damage on the well-being of the nation as a whole. In particular, the regular export of large amounts of bullion suggested to many that the Company was draining the country of much of its wealth, and the practice was to be condemned for many years to come. Such a serious charge called into question the whole point and purpose of the East India trade, and the Company was obliged to mount a sustained propaganda campaign in defence of its monopoly and trading practices. Friends and allies rallied to the cause, most notably Thomas Mun, the mercantilist author who wrote detailed analyses of the Company's trade and enumerated the direct and indirect benefits that were brought to the country as a whole. Mun was robust in his defence of the export of bullion, a position he set out most effectively in his influential pamphlet of 1621 entitled *A Discourse of Trade from England unto the East Indies*.

The arguments of Mun and others helped to keep the Company's critics at bay, even if they were not silenced altogether. Indeed, the Company was never wholly secure, and the continuing weaknesses in its domestic position were revealed during the 1640s and 1650s when it was buffeted by the extreme political and economic turbulence caused by the English Civil War and the Interregnum. Caught in the cross-fire between the Royalists and Parliamentarians, and with its own ranks divided along political lines, the future of the Company often looked very bleak, never more so than in 1653 when the Lord Protector, Oliver Cromwell, decided not to renew the Company's charter, thereby allowing free adventurers to have access to Eastern markets. This opening up of trade created something of a free-for-all which proved to be disastrous for English interests in Asia as private traders competed aggressively with one another, and it brought no obvious benefits to either the merchant community or the state. In fact, the whole rather sorry episode underlined that a well-regulated joint-stock monopoly enterprise backed by the state still represented the most effective way of organising English trade in the Indian Ocean. After much reflection, Cromwell performed a volte-face and in 1657 sanctioned the full restoration of the Company's exclusive privileges; a surge in investor confidence was reflected in the large sum of £786,000 that was very quickly subscribed to a new joint stock. This in itself was important, but equally so was the fact that the new joint stock was deemed to be permanent, an arrangement that signalled for the first time that the Company had a secure long-term future.

CONSOLIDATION AND COMMERCIAL GROWTH

It is not surprising that in view of the difficulties experienced at home and abroad the Company's commercial performance was erratic during the first half of the 17th century. This was reflected in the profits generated for investors, and it proved impossible to sustain the very healthy rates of return enjoyed before 1620. The second joint stock of 1617–32 made a profit of only 12 per cent.[5] Although things then improved as the third joint stock earned 35 per cent between 1631 and 1642, the Company's financial situation was often parlous, and this led to periodic bouts of cost-cutting and retrenchment, which hindered the growth of the Company as an institution. It was only when organisational stability coincided with the political stability that returned to England with the restoration of the monarchy in 1660 that the Company could more fully concentrate its attention on consolidating its trading network and refining the maritime system in order to increase the flow of goods from Asia.

The pattern of commercial operations that emerged during the second half of the 17th century was quite different from that envisaged by the

Company's founding fathers. Change had become evident during the difficult times of the 1620s and 1630s, when the factory at Surat gradually supplanted Bantam as the main hub of the Company's trading operation. There was still a need to supply saleable commodities to the factors in the Spice Islands, but Indian goods now became much more prominent in the return cargoes sent to England. The Company first imported cottons into London in 1613, when 5,000 pieces were put up for auction. By the 1620s, four generic types of cloth were being sold on a regular basis: plain white calicoes, single coloured cloths, striped chintzes, and the painted cloths known as pintadoes. In addition, the Company also began to import bulk shipments of indigo, saltpetre and sugar, as well as coffee purchased at Mocha. This process was accompanied by a broadening of the Company's geographical presence in India, and commercial activity began to be conducted in the textile-rich region of Bengal, where a permanent factory was first established at Hughli in 1651 (fig.15). The quantity of pepper procured by the Company (now from the Malabar Coast in India as well as the East Indies) was still very considerable, with annual imports peaking at eight million pounds in

fig.15
The Town of Huley,
by Edward Barlow, 17th century
The East India Company established a factory at Hughli in 1651, in order to access the rich textile markets of Bengal.
[JOD/4/109, detail]

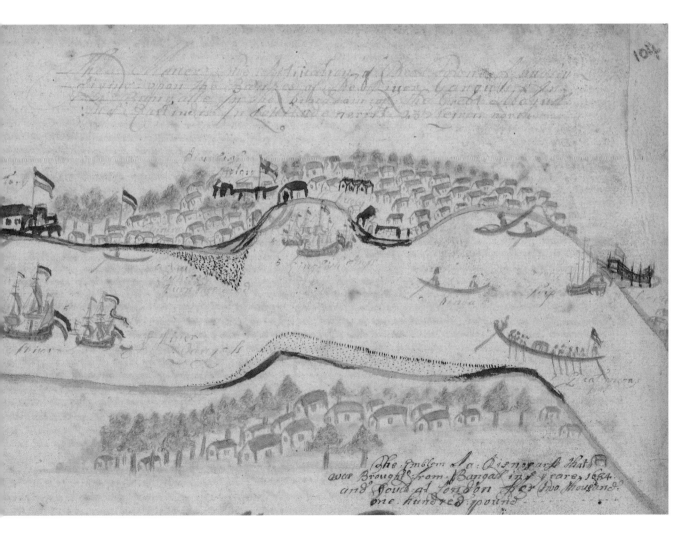

1677. While there continued to be undimmed interest in the major spices, the Company's attention was increasingly focused on cotton.[6]

The rate of growth of the Company's textile trade was far from uniform, but by 1664 cottons accounted for over 70 per cent of the value of all imports, and a greater range of products began to be procured for sale in London and re-export markets. At times, huge quantities of cloth were imported and during the early 1680s, for example, the Company ordered over two million pieces of cloth a year. Much of this cloth was of a basic functional type, but a great variety of fine coloured and plain cottons, as well as silks, increasingly found favour with the middling and upper orders in English society. Demand strengthened as people sought to use cottons for clothing as well as bed linen and decorative wall hangings, and the Company became well attuned to the need to respond to prevailing fashion. Accordingly, close attention was paid to the weight, colour, pattern and texture of the cloth required by domestic consumers, and detailed procurement instructions were sent to the factors in India. This had the desired effect as far as sales in London were concerned, and contemporary observers noted the onset of a calico 'craze' in England. As one writer explained in 1699:

It was scarce thought about twenty years since that we should ever see Calicoes the ornaments of our greatest Gallants (for such they are whether we call them Muslins, Shades, or anything else) when they were then rarely used ... but now few think themselves well dresst till they are made up in Calicoes, both men and women, Calico Shirts, Neckcloths, Cuffs, Pocket-handkerchiefs for the former, Head-Dresses, Nightroyls, Hoods, Sleeves, Aprons, Gowns, Petticoats, and what not for the latter, beside India stockings for both sexes.[7]

The foundations of the Company's long-term commercial success were being built upon an expanding trade in Indian textiles, but other commodities began to be imported into London for the first time. Looking to the future, the most significant development was the trade in tea, although it was some considerable time before the Company was able to establish regular direct links with the Chinese port of Canton. Before then, the Company often acquired tea through the actions of its merchants at Madras, who were able to secure small consignments through the country trade. Hence, although the diarist Samuel Pepys first tasted tea during the 1660s, it was not for several decades that supplies to London became organised on a regular basis (fig.16). Even then, tea did not contribute much to the overall value of imports until after 1711, when the Company was able to gain regular access to Canton. Nonetheless, an increasing thirst for tea in England strengthened an already existing fascination for 'chinoiserie' or luxury and semi-luxury items from China and elsewhere. Tea equipment and furniture were especially in demand, and the Company responded by importing

fig.16
Teapot, late 17th century
Tea was one of the most lucrative commodities brought back to Europe for sale by the Company. Before leaving Asia, consignments of tea were tested on the quayside in small teapots such as this one.
[AAA6188]

chinaware or porcelain and lacquerware furnishings of various types. As a result, by the end of the 17th century, the Company's trade had become a cornerstone of English overseas trade, and it had contributed to changes in long-term patterns of consumption which altered quite fundamentally the ways in which people in Britain ate, drank, dressed and, indeed, behaved.

The strengthening and expansion of Company trade after 1650 is evident from the increasing number of ships dispatched to Asia each year. During the 1640s, 45 ships had sailed to the East, and 52 were sent out in the following decade. Thereafter, the growing scale of Company trade was marked: 94 ships went to Asia during the 1660s, 145 in the 1670s, and 139 in the 1680s. Supporting this maritime activity posed many organisational challenges, and as with everything else to do with the Company, it took some time for a fully mature shipping 'system' to evolve. For example, after purchasing ships for its early voyages the Company decided to build and repair its own vessels, which led it to develop two major dockyards on the River Thames. In 1607, it leased the Deptford Yard, near Greenwich, where ships were built to the same standards as naval vessels; five years later land was purchased on the Isle of Dogs at Blackwall where a repair yard was constructed. By 1618, over 200 men were working at Blackwall Yard and the Company had become one of the largest employers of civilian labour in London. Yet shipbuilding proved to be a very costly business because of its high overheads, and when economies had to be made during the 1630s the Company also began to hire ships. As a result, the lease on Deptford Yard was given up, and Blackwall Yard was eventually sold in 1656. Thereafter, the Company routinely hired ships from small consortia of private owners, and this practice continued until 1833 (fig.17).

fig.17 *(overleaf)*
East India Company Ships at Deptford,
English school, *c.*1660
In 1607, the Company decided to build its own ships and they leased a yard in Deptford, near Greenwich, for this purpose. The striped ensigns identify these as Company ships. Later in the century, the Company reverted to hiring vessels, many of which were built in the private yards at Deptford and Blackwall.
[BHC1873]

fig.18
*Two Views of an East Indiaman
of the Time of King William III,
by Isaac Sailmaker, c.1685*
This traditional ship portrait shows
two views of the same East India
ship: on the left is a broadside view;
on the right the ship is depicted
from astern. The vessel is heavily
armed, mounting over 60 guns.
The flag at the stern identifies it
as a Company ship.

[BHC1676]

fig.19
Model of the East Indiaman
Somerset, 1738
This is one of the oldest models
of an East India ship in existence.
It is built on a scale of 1:48. The
Somerset was about 148½ feet long
and 32 feet in the beam. At
around 950 tons, it had a crew
of about 100 men and carried
between 50 and 60 guns. The
Somerset made two trading voyages
to India between 1738 and 1748.

[SLR0452]

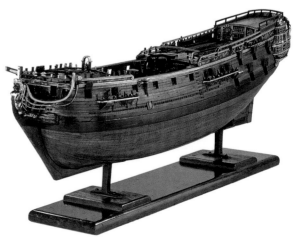

In the Company's early days, some of its ships were very large indeed. For example the aptly named *Trades Increase*, launched at Deptford by James I in 1609, was a huge vessel of 1,239 tons. Over time, however, experience and changing conditions dictated that ships became rather smaller in size, with standard design 500- to 800-ton vessels being the norm until after 1780, when a rapid expansion of the tea trade led to a need for the Company to use larger 1,200-ton and even 1,400-ton ships once more. It was these smaller types of ships that later became known to contemporaries as 'East Indiamen', and they were to symbolise the growing strength of Britain's maritime presence in the Indian Ocean (figs 18 and 19).

Voyages to Asia remained long, difficult and dangerous, and Company ships were always dependent upon transit islands and stopping places where stocks of water, fruit, vegetables and animals could be replenished. They were also important as places where passengers and crew could recuperate from illness, disease and exhaustion. Moreover, sea passages to the East were determined by the movement of tide and wind, and this took Company ships along standard routes that meant certain places were visited on a regular basis. On outward voyages, ships often touched at Madeira, Teneriffe, the Cape Verde Islands, Brazil and, especially, the Cape of Good Hope. On leaving the Cape, the route taken by a ship depended on its ultimate destination. Those heading to western and southern India often took the 'inner passage' through the Mozambique Channel, where they called at Madagascar or the Comoro Islands, before they picked up the south-westerly monsoon winds. On the other hand, ships sailing straight to Bengal, the East Indies and China, sailed directly eastward from the Cape well out into the southern Indian Ocean before turning northwards, with those heading to Canton having to negotiate difficult passages through the straits of the Indonesian Archipelago. The pattern and length of return voyages meant that most homeward-bound ships stopped at St Helena, the South Atlantic island that passed into the possession of the Company in 1659 and became a linchpin in the Company's shipping operation (figs 20 and 21).

fig. 20
Sea chest, *c.*1820
East India Company servants travelling to live and work in Asia could bring very few luxuries or home comforts with them on their long sea voyages. The contents of one chest like this might be the limit of their possessions.

[AAA3322]

fig. 21
Shipping off Saint Helena,
by Adam Callander, *c.*1780
Situated in the South Atlantic near
the Tropic of Capricorn, St Helena
is 1,200 miles from the west coast of
Africa and 1,800 miles from Brazil.
It was a regular watering and supply
station, and convoy rendezvous, for
sailing vessels bound to and from
the East Indies via the Cape of
Good Hope.

[BHC1926]

out and about 6 weekes After, Receud my waiges for the Iuie I found in this Cuy the ben
Called the Jent of no Greter power then one hundred and io Joine did not Tho after my arivel I stad
a Mays Sitt & Sickenese but it pleased the al mightie to Returne to my health againe and when the
Receud my waiges I had Thus to peticion to the Company to Jee that Recompence toud Col. Johnson
my selfe and Bove Son to me to Jead I mith But Tous Col Johnson then but Toud me I must Go
Egile Low of him I hoad and the neat Jeaindicatum I tould haue of the Company the ben the
only pensone that Jee at Errance decontik emong them that Jerued them and to ij The Red many
to haue Spent in Lem i might haue Recoured Som Right til hauing non mush Set Downe wi th arti
partiance praying to God in this for him to Reuen me Jaure for might did euer Lom Right Sonot
Long afterward the wore tould thi ho the Lord was Guen me again to the Conuen to Go for East India
hauing a new Comander Put in her which had Carryd the former Supand as a dead which did in ij
Jrilla and to Jaiec with him Go Loe in the Ship againe to Indja hauing only io Sildrene the
Month more then Tha Commin tour and hauing at tom Cul the Later end of nouember it pleased god
to Cal to him left a Mall Dauchter of min which was Born a Loint Sim befor I went out tho waige
Before it being a Great Grest Cow Bothe til we night Co Submit Co the will of the Lord for hee did
thawethe what it Good for us and Setting our Ship il Lenh no Sea or ros Co loe for Surral in east
India Tho Pendringes More goy on Bord of us then only Three Childs and a Barell of John
Melle and 10000 ipeund, in Cash Co in the qth Day of december hauing all thing en Bord the
tho Sgile we Sett Sail from Graues and tho Ship wee are being Sick 5 Dayes Before are and with
we Sail Two Ships from Graues in the Lendast and the thresbury but wee were Bound
Co Bangal Before we Got in Co the Downe we met with the winde Easterly But in Three
Dayes Cittle wee Got in to thel Downe Finding no Shippe ther but only the Dartmuth Frigat which
Fired a Gun at us Becaus we did not Lower our Copsaile Go her a Long tim Before we Cam nere to
her Co Comin Co enter and hauing Hajreowine Jent our Bot ashor for the Boying Som fresh
prouisions Co Carey wi thus and it Cor 7 howres Sim we weia Gone and Set Sail out of the downs

Those running the Company's affairs always recognised the strategic importance of maintaining unrestricted access to places such as St Helena and the Cape.

As the Company built up its trade and maritime infrastructure during the second half of the 17th century, it also consolidated its network of factories in Asia. In the East Indies, the English were finally expelled from Bantam by the Dutch in 1682. But they were still eager to secure pepper supplies in the region, and they responded to this setback three years later by creating a new factory at Bengkulu on the west coast of Sumatra. This factory, which became Fort Marlborough in 1714, was destined to be a backwater, and far more attention was paid to strengthening the Company's position in India. Surat was to remain important as a commercial gateway to northern textile markets, but the Company gradually derived benefit from the acquisition of several key settlements that began to serve as administrative centres and were eventually to mature into the three 'presidencies' of Bombay, Calcutta and Madras. The process, which slowly came to mark out the main contours of the Company's later empire in India, began in 1639 when the Company was granted the right to construct Fort St George at Madras on the Coromandel Coast (figs 22 and 23). It continued in 1668 when the Company acquired Bombay, which had been granted by the Portuguese to Charles II as part of his marriage settlement of 1661. Bombay island had much to commend it since its location offered security and an excellent harbour. But it initially remained underdeveloped as a commercial centre, not least because powerful Indian merchants, especially those of the Parsee community, refused to relocate there from Surat. Finally, in 1690, Job Charnock acquired three small villages in Bengal that were to develop into the town of Calcutta. In 1696, the fortification of this new settlement was undertaken as the English sought to protect themselves during a local insurrection. The new trading station was formally given the name Fort William in 1700 and, although Calcutta was still a long way from being the 'City of Palaces' it later became, the nature of this new establishment in the rich Mughal province of Bengal symbolised how much the Company had changed over the course of its first hundred years.

fig. 22
Fort St George, by Edward Barlow, 17th century
Fort St George was established by the East India Company on the west coast of India in 1639.
[JOD/4/110]

fig. 23 *(overleaf)*
Fort St George on the Coromandel Coast, after Jan van Ryne, 1754
The fort, and the city of Madras that developed around it, became one of the Company's most important trading stations in India in the 18th century.
[PAD1845]

2

Places far remote ... cause much expectation
Encounters and diplomacy in Asia,
1600–1800

JOHN MCALEER

Before the establishment of the East India Company, British ideas about Asia and its people were based on the experience of the overland trade with the Levant. With the development of maritime trading routes around the Cape of Good Hope in the 15th century, a new world of commercial possibilities presented itself to European travellers. Company representatives met and did business with a variety of African and Asian people. They experienced, at first hand, the societies and landscapes of the vast region bordering what Thomas Cavendish described as 'that mighty and vast sea'.[1] From southern Africa, the Swahili Coast and Arabia to India, China and Japan, European sailors and merchants came into contact with people, places and things that were entirely new to them. Travellers examined social customs, language, material production, eating habits and religious beliefs. Their remarks expressed fascination, admiration and sometimes bemusement at the sites and situations presented to them as a result of trade with the East.

Of course, European maritime interest in, and knowledge of, Asia preceded the foundation of the trading companies. Sir Francis Drake, for example, crossed the Indian Ocean on his circumnavigation of the globe in the 1570s. When he and his men called at the Moluccas, Drake sent a messenger to the king with a velvet cloak as a token of his peaceful intentions. The king responded in similar fashion, dispatching four large canoes, carrying dignitaries 'attired in white lawn cloth of Calicut'. They rowed past the English 'with great solemnity'. Elsewhere in the Moluccas, at 'Barateve' (now Bacan), Drake and his companions found the people 'comely in body and stature, and of a civil behaviour, just in dealing, and courteous to strangers'. The landscape of the island was also a subject of admiration. It was 'rich and beautiful: rich in gold, silver, copper, and sulphur'. Nutmeg, ginger, pepper, lemons, cucumbers and coconuts were in plentiful supply, so much so that 'since the time that we first set out of our own country of England, we happened on no place, wherein we found more comforts and better means of refreshing'.[2]

Following the establishment of the East India Company in London in 1600, many more travellers were drawn to Asia, remarking on its peoples, places and commercial prospects in the process. One of the most important early visitors was Sir Thomas Roe (fig. 24). He was well qualified to provide a lively and interesting account of his experiences because, even in his student days in the Middle Temple, Roe was renowned as a sparkling conversationalist and raconteur. In many ways, his career characterises the global connections of early Jacobean England. In 1607, he was appointed to the Royal Council of Virginia, subsequently becoming a substantial investor in the young colony. In February 1610, Roe commanded an expedition to Guinea, in South America, in search of Manoa, capital of the legendary

Thys doth ye baker and shoales and small jlands on the north west syde of ye
Marregather or sant lorrance shew   SSWS 9 Leagues   SSWSt
them so dais at ye topmast hed we being
then in 14 fadam water on ye
latitude of 12 degrees south

SSE 3 Leagues

Sy n 5 Leagues

A Mape of The Sittuation of The port and Ride of Carmarcongine
lying upon The Malebarr coast in the East Indie in the Lattitude of 14 degrees
and 30 Minutes north, with the jland of Ingedeua where goods bought
m Easter December 1608

The Clerone of Carmare

62

priest-king El Dorado. In October 1614, following these forays in the Atlantic Ocean, Roe accepted an invitation from the East India Company to become England's first ambassador to Mughal India. He would spend three years travelling in India, providing one of the earliest accounts in English of the colour and exuberance of Asia and confirming his opinion that 'places far remote … cause much expectation'.[3] For Roe and his companions, Asia seemed to be the stuff of fables. So unusual and interesting was his time at the court of the Mughal emperor, Jahángír, that he wrote to George Abbot, the Archbishop of Canterbury, that 'a description of the land, customs, and manners, with other accidents, are fitter for winter nights' when tall tales would be told around hearth fires.[4]

Edward Barlow was another traveller whose remarks on the people and places he encountered in Asia provide a valuable record of the early days of the Company and the people who served with it. Barlow had more adventures than most, serving in eight East India Company ships between 1669 and 1703. In keeping a journal of his life 'below decks', Barlow provides a contrast to Roe's time amid the regal splendour of the Mughal court. Born near Manchester, Barlow went to London in 1657 to live with an uncle who ran the *Dog and Bear* hostelry at Southwark. Connections in the Navy Office secured young Barlow an apprenticeship aboard the *Naseby*, the ship that carried Charles II back from Holland at the Restoration. As East India Company trade opened up opportunities for greater travel in the late 17th century, Barlow eagerly grasped the chance 'to see strange countries'.[5] He even accepted less than the 26 shillings a month he earned in the Navy to take a position in a Company vessel. In 1670, Barlow made his first voyage to the East Indies, sailing to Bombay, Surat and Malabar aboard the *Experiment* (fig. 25).

Roe and Barlow, and many others besides, initially recorded their impressions as sailors. Maritime commerce facilitated personal interaction. Navigating across the Indian Ocean, and passing the ports and people around its shores, these travellers encountered the complex trading networks of Asia at first hand. Their experiences laid the foundations for the ways in which Europeans would view the Indian Ocean world for centuries.

FIRST IMPRESSIONS

It could take up to six months and longer for ships to reach the spice and textile markets of Asia. The absolute necessity of stopping to acquire supplies en route ensured that any area offering respite to travellers and provisions for the journey was welcome. Africa provided the most obvious stopping-off points and victualling stations for East India Company fleets.

fig. 25
The Malabar Coast, by Edward Barlow, 17th century
The south-western coast of India was one of the most important locations for maritime trade in Asia.
[JOD/4/71]

Even before Company ships plied the route, Francis Drake had passed the Cape of Good Hope in June 1580 on the homeward leg of his voyage around the world. For Drake and his crew, it presented a wholesome and attractive location: 'This Cape is a most stately thing, and the fairest Cape we saw in the whole circumference of the earth.'[6] With its bays, inlets and fertile hinterland, the peninsula at the Cape of Good Hope became a crucial landmark for East India ships over the centuries, with the Dutch establishing a supply station there in 1652 (fig. 26). It was a gateway to the Indian Ocean world, its markets and commercial possibilities. Sir Edward Michelborne found 'a goodly Country' in 1605, providing abundant quantities of meat for sailors, who were more accustomed to living on the most meagre rations of dry biscuit and brackish water.[7] According to Nicholas Downton in 1610, the Cape was a place which had always been 'comfortable to all our nation travelling this way, both outwards and homewards, yielding them abundance of flesh, as sheep and beef'.[8]

fig. 26
Plate, 18th century
This Chinese porcelain plate shows a fleet of Dutch ships at anchor in Table Bay, South Africa. European ships travelling to Asia needed safe and convenient stations en route, where they could take on fresh food and supplies.

[AAA4453]

ENCOUNTERS AND DIPLOMACY IN ASIA, 1600–1800

Despite these positive portents, Thomas Roe's first encounter with Africa could have been disastrous. The fleet in which he was travelling almost went aground near Cape Bojador, on the African mainland south of the Canaries. In a near-fatal example of the navigational limitations of the time, the Cape had been incorrectly placed by 60 miles in their charts. Having overcome this, the party eventually arrived at the Cape of Good Hope, where they erected five tents on shore and spent a fortnight on land. Roe's journal provides a colourful account of their time there, and some of the first European observations of the indigenous inhabitants. Roe found them to be:

[t]he most barbarous in the world, eating carrion, wearing the guts of sheep about their necks for health, and rubbing their heads (curled like negroes) with dung of beasts and dirt. They have no other clothing than beasts' skins wrapped on their shoulders, their skin next the body in heat, in cold the hairy side ... They know no kind of God or religion.[9]

Edward Barlow also found the local 'Hottentots' less than civilised, describing them as 'the heathenest people that I have seen, neither knowing good and worshipping neither God or Devil, going about more like brute beasts than mortal men, and [eating] any raw flesh or guts of beasts which are thrown away'.[10] Views such as those expressed by Barlow and Roe reflect the ways in which early European travellers filtered their responses to non-European people through their own social and religious frames of reference.

Of course, the objective of most Company ships in this period was to make their way to the Spice Islands or to India. The Dutch and the Portuguese were the first Europeans to establish themselves in these regions. By the end of the 16th century, the Portuguese colony of Goa on the west coast of India was the largest European-ruled city in Asia. As capital of the Portuguese vice-kingdom there, the other Portuguese possessions in Asia were under the suzerainty of its viceroy. This street scene in Goa (fig. 27) was first published in Jan Huyghen van Linschoten's *Itinerario*. Linschoten was a Dutch traveller who published an account of his travels in the Portuguese East Indies in the 1590s. The print illustrates the houses of the city's Rua Direita as well as the variety of people who lived there, attracted by the money-making possibilities offered by a busy trading port. Ralph Fitch, a London merchant who visited Goa in the 1580s, thought it was a 'fine city', 'very fair, full of orchards and gardens, and many palm trees'. Nevertheless, in an indication of the mistrust and commercial rivalries that existed between competing European countries at the time, Fitch was charged with being a spy and thrown in prison when he arrived there.[11] The *Hector* was the first English ship to drop anchor in India. It arrived at Surat, further up the west coast, in 1608 on the third East India Company voyage to Asia. Here too, the Portuguese guarded their commercial advantages zealously. According to William Biddulph, the East India Company's 'factor' or representative there, they 'use all the means they possibly can to root us out of this place, which is the only place for vending our country's commodities that is in all the Indies, and for commodities for England'.[12]

As Europeans exploited the commercial potential of Asian trade they also commented more generally on the people they encountered on their way there, and their perceived state of 'civilisation' and morals. In describing the indigenous inhabitants of the Nicobar Islands, a traveller on the first East India Company voyage pronounced 'these people of the east are wholly given to deceit'. The Javans, in particular, were 'reckoned among the greatest pickers and thieves of the world'.[13] As Roe's remarks indicate, Africans were particularly poorly regarded. In July 1620, Captains Andrew Shillinge and Humphrey Fitzherbert landed at what they believed to be 'Saldanha Bay'

fig. 27
Street scene in Goa, engraved by **Johannes Doetechum,** 1599
European East India Companies often established fortified trading stations, or 'factories', in Asia. Goa, on the west coast of India and controlled by the Portuguese, was one of the first of these and developed into an important trading centre.

[PAI0227]

O Leilaõ. que se faz cada dia pola menhã na Rua direita na Cidade de Goa Feito Polo natural. por Ioan de Linschoten framengo.

Xaraffo Wisselaer

Porteiro Wtroeper

Pingues Arbeiders

Ama Voester

Sande

Goënsi se quanta foro viden area pandat
Plana frequens tectis splendida dives opum?

Vt mercem hic properet gemmis auroque nitentem
Ille abducta procul vendere mancipia?

Congesta huc videa
Insulę et Eoo

ENCOUNTERS AND DIPLOMACY IN ASIA, 1600–1800

(in reality, Table Bay) and claimed it for King James. They considered the inhabitants to be 'but naked men and without an Head or policy'.[14] At Madagascar, a nascent English settlement was abandoned after barely a year in May 1646, with the original 140 settlers delighted to leave this 'most accursed place'. The settlers found the natives to be 'of so base and false a condition that they have not their fellows in the whole world'.[15]

Opinions about Indians varied. Thomas Roe concluded that they had 'almost no civil acts, but such as straggling Christians have lately taught them'.[16] But Sir William Norris, nearly a century later, had better experiences. Over the course of a three-month stay at Masulipatam in 1699, he had 'neither seen nor heard of any drunkenness, disorder, riot or quarrelling in the Town'. He remarked that it 'would be well if European City's [*sic*] would take example'.[17] Edward Barlow also described the places

A. *Misericordia*

Joannes à Doetechum fecit.

: portat et *Indus* | *Fori Goensis tabernarum mercium et mer-* | *Claere opdoeninge vande merckt van Goa*
Occano. | *catorum illud frequentantium aperta ex-* | *met haer winckelen waren in daegelickse*
Hoogerh. | *plicatio per N.Linschoten* | *Coopluyden. door I. H. V. Linschoten* | *44 en 45*

and people he came into contact with. At Bombay (fig. 28), he found the people to be 'naturally black and tawny':

Their religion is not well known, they worshipping all manner of images, and the sun and the moon, yet they live very peaceably under the English, enjoying all their old customs and privileges … Their women go strangely attired, wearing rings with pearls and other precious stones in their noses and ears, and arms and legs, having suchlike things in great value about them.

On the Malabar Coast, by contrast, the inhabitants were reported 'to worship the Devil for their God, and every Friday to offer one of their children to him'. The people of Madras worshipped 'idols and cows and beads, as all other East Indians do, but are generally a very civil people, as those of Bengal are, to strangers'.[18]

Barlow's travels took him as far as China, where he found the people to be 'all heathens, worshipping several sorts of idols and images': 'The shape of a dragon is in great request and much honoured by them.' He commented

fig. 28
Bombay, by Edward Barlow,
17th century
The Portuguese initially controlled the land around what became Bombay. However, when Catherine of Braganza married King Charles II, it formed part of her dowry. In 1668, the Crown leased Bombay to the East India Company for a sum of £10 per annum.

[JOD/4/69]

fig. 29
Macao, by Edward Barlow,
17th century
Macao developed as a settlement in the 16th century, when Portuguese merchants obtained trading rights there. In 1557, the Portuguese established a permanent settlement in Macao, paying an annual rent of 500 *taels* of silver to the Chinese.

[JOD/4/136]

fig. 30
Canton, by Edward Barlow,
17th century
The Portuguese were the first Europeans to arrive in Canton by sea in the early 16th century. The city quickly became the most important Chinese port for European trading.

[JOD/4/139]

on their physical appearance ('an indifferent fair complexion'), their hair styles ('all of them wear their hair long, never cutting it so long as they live'), and their fashion accessories ('The better sort of them, both men and women, carry fans in their hands and parasols over their heads to keep the heat and sun from them in summer time.') (figs 29 and 30).[19] Jean-Baptiste Du Halde, a French Jesuit historian who collated descriptions of China, found that 'there is no nation more proud of their pretended grandeur'. The Chinese were 'so full of their own country, customs, manners, and maxims, that they cannot be persuaded there is any good thing out of China, or any truth but what their learned men are acquainted with'. He questioned their sincerity: 'Honesty is not their favourite virtue; especially when they have to do with strangers, whom they seldom fail to cheat, and brag of it.' Du Halde acknowledged, however, that visiting European merchants might have inspired such behaviour as 'it is said that some Europeans have taught them their trade'.[20] Others also found the Chinese difficult to do business

ENCOUNTERS AND DIPLOMACY IN ASIA, 1600–1800

with. A trader aboard the *Macclesfield*, the first English ship to trade successfully at Canton, recounted:

The many troubles and vexations we have met with from these subtle Chinese — whose principles allow them to cheat, and their daily practice therein have made them dextrous at it — I am not able to express at this time; and how ever easy others may have represented the trade of China, neither I nor my Assistants have found it so, for every day produces new troubles.[21]

Whatever his misgivings about the ordinary inhabitants of India, Thomas Roe was thoroughly impressed by the theatrical splendour and spectacle of the Mughal court there. His diary recorded an audience with Jahángír (fig.31), who wore 'more jewels than any other monarch in the world'. The emperor sat on a throne raised four feet above the floor with seven oil paintings arranged behind him. Roe thought it was one of the most magnificent sights he had ever seen:

The King sits in a little gallery over head; ambassadors, the great men and strangers of quality within the inmost rail under him, raised from the ground, covered with canopies of velvet and silk, under foot laid with good carpets … The sitting so hath so much affinity with a theatre — the manner of the King in his gallery; the great men lifted on a stage as actors; the vulgar below gazing on.

He continued by commenting on Jahángír's territories, which were 'far greater than the Persians, and almost equal, if not as great as, the Turks'.[22] Confirming Roe's opinion, William Hawkins, commander of the *Hector*, also outlined the extent of Jahángír's control:

The compass of his country is two years travel with Caravan, to say, from Candahar to Agra, from Loughtare in Bengal to Agra, from Cabul to Agra, from Deccan to Agra, from Surat to Agra, from Tatta in Sinde to Agra. Agra is in a manner in the heart of all his Kingdoms.

According to Hawkins's account, 'this King is thought to be the greatest Emperor of the East, for Wealth, Land, and force of Men: as also for Horses, Elephants, Camels and Dromedaries'. He also provided an exhaustive list of the kinds of treasure possessed by the Great Mughal, which he divided according to type: 'Coin of Gold', 'Coin of Silver', 'his Jewels of all Sorts', 'Jewels wrought in Gold', and 'all sorts of Beasts'.[23] Even in this exalted presence, misunderstandings could occur. An incident involving an exquisite miniature, which Thomas Roe presented to Jahángír as a gift, indicated some of the tensions that these encounters between Europeans and Asians created. Wagering that he could distinguish the original from any copy that Jahángír's court artists might make, Roe underestimated the skill of the local artists. The emperor was delighted when Roe proved to have great difficulty as this would show people 'in England [that] we are not so unskilful as you esteem us'.[24]

fig.31
The Emperor Jahángír Receiving his Second Son, Prince Parviz, in Audience, c.1614
Jahángír was the ruler of the Mughal Empire from 1605 until his death in 1627. His name means 'Conqueror of the World' in Persian. In order to trade freely in India, Europeans had to get permission from him.
[V&A Museum]

One of the fundamental building blocks of communication – language – was a particularly difficult obstacle for Europeans to overcome. Although the East India Company often sent letters to Asian rulers written in English or Latin, the *lingua franca* of the Indian Ocean world was Arabic, with Persian also widely employed.[25] Linguistic difficulties not only hindered communication but, in the event of an untrustworthy interpreter being employed, they could also undermine the entire expedition. At one point during his time at the Mughal court, Roe had to speak broken Spanish to an Italian translator who rendered it in Turkish for a Safavid prince, who then translated it into Persian for the courtiers. At the same time, however, language could be a powerful catalyst for increased interaction and mutual understanding. As Roe struggled with court protocol, for example, Edward Terry's enquiring mind and linguistic ability enabled him to compile a valuable account of the entire Mughal dominions and their varied inhabitants. He was engaged by the East India Company to act as Roe's chaplain and, in February 1616, he sailed in the flagship of the fleet. Terry found Hindustani 'a smooth tongue and easy to be pronounced'.[26] He also learned Persian and some Arabic. But Terry was in the minority, and it was not until later in the century that Europeans made a concerted effort to equip themselves with the necessary linguistic skills to do business with Asians more successfully.

In order to achieve this, the Company began to send out apprentices to learn the basics of the local language before they entered employment with them. In 1735, for example, a boy called James Flint was sent to Canton to learn the local dialect and thereby facilitate trade. Relationships with local women and just listening to Asians made linguists of others. By the early 18th century, the study of Oriental languages – generally Hebrew, Persian and Arabic – was becoming an established discipline in European universities. In 1734, George Sale published an English version of the Qur'an. As trade became more important, so Europeans took ever-greater interest in the people with whom they were likely to be doing business. Of course, increased trade also meant that there was more to lose, and more urgency to make a good impression on the local ruler.

THE RETURN VOYAGE: ASIA COMES TO EUROPE

Just as East India Company ships brought more Europeans to Asian shores, so Asians also travelled to Europe in greater numbers. An example of this is the embassy sent to London by the ruler of Bantam, a kingdom near the northern extremity of the Sunda Straits and which, in the 16th century, covered large parts of western Java and southern Sumatra. The city of Bantam occupied a crucial strategic location linking the Indian Ocean with the China Seas. Furthermore, its pepper crops had attracted European interest from the earliest days of the trading companies. James Lancaster visited the city in 1602, establishing an English factory there. Fifty miles to the east, the Dutch founded Batavia in 1619. Conscious of the simmering rivalry between these two powers, the Sultan of Bantam was keen to exploit this in order to consolidate his own position. He wanted to cement relations with the English, whom he felt would provide a bulwark and ally against possible Dutch ambitions. The specific objective of the London mission was to get consent from King Charles II for the export of large ordnance. The sultan sent two ambassadors, together with significant amounts of pepper and rough diamonds, worth £1,600, for presentation to the king. They arrived at Erith in the *New London* in April 1682 and were received with all the pomp attendant on a royal visit. On 9 May 1682, *The London Gazette* reported that they had made their 'publick entry, having been received and complimented at Greenwich'. After this, the party was taken 'from thence by water in His Majesties [*sic*] barge to Tower-Hill', where they were 'saluted with the great guns', and then taken in the royal coach to a house prepared for them at Charing Cross. They were subsequently received at Windsor and took part in a series of engagements, one of which was a performance of Shakespeare's *The Tempest* at the Duke's Theatre.[27]

East India ships did not just bring back goods for sale. When Thomas Roe returned to Europe in the 900-ton *Royal Anne*, the ship's cargo of indigo, cotton goods and Persian silk was augmented by the Emperor Jahángír's gifts for King James. Roe carried his own acquisitions too: a great Indian cabinet for his wife, a green embroidered bed with matching quilts, and a large carpet woven with the family coat-of-arms. While the principal goal of the East India Company was to increase trade and maximise profit, the expansion of knowledge was also perceived as a significant benefit. The scientist Robert Boyle, an early supporter of the Company, claimed that his interest in Asia was inspired by 'the desire of knowledge, not profit'. He received letters from natural philosophers bound for India who pondered on their new surroundings, and reported on climate, weather, plants, animals, medicines, magical stones, curious people, customs and religion.[28] Following his return from Ceylon, Robert Knox was called before the East India Company's Court of Directors to give an account of his travels. Among other things, Knox brought a leaf of the tallipot tree back to England, to demonstrate how it was used as an umbrella by the Ceylonese. Later he also presented exotic plants and seeds of various types to Robert Hooke of the Royal Society, including cannabis and wood from the Mascarene islands of Mauritius and Rodrigues ('Diego Rois').

Collectible curiosities, as well as the exotic animals and plants of Asia, were highly sought after in Europe. The 'King of Achem' sent a letter to

fig. 32

Elephant, by Edward Barlow,
17th century

As well as commercial goods and
luxury objects, some of the most
sought-after Asian items were
strange and exotic animals.

[JOD/4/116, detail]

Queen Elizabeth expressing fraternal respect and sending, by the hands of
Lancaster, 'a ring of gold beautified with a ruby, richly placed in his set, two
vestures woven with gold, embroidered with gold, inclosed in a red box of
tzin [*sic*]'.[29] Exotic Asian animals were highly prized expressions of luxury
and majesty in European aristocratic circles (fig. 32). The Portuguese led
the way, with Manuel I (reigned 1495–1521) parading five elephants through
the streets of Lisbon. Others followed suit, particularly with larger ships
providing greater storage capacity. In 1607, the Earl of Salisbury applied for
leave to send someone to bring home 'paratts, munkies, and marmasitts'. As
a result, the commander of the third Company voyage was duly instructed to
bring back the creatures mentioned 'or other strange beasts and fowls that
you esteem rare and delightful'. In the instructions given to Lawrence Femell,
the principal factor on the sixth Company voyage, he was also ordered to
procure 'any rare things', such as birds or animals, 'fit to present to His
Majesty or to the Noble Lords that are the Company's friends'. Sir Henry
Middleton, the commander, was similarly charged to look out for likely gifts.
If he came across any he was to send them home to the committee 'in the
charge of careful persons'. And, furthermore, if he knew 'of any of the
mariners to possess such [animals], and to refuse to part with [them],
he is to inform the committee, who will take steps accordingly'.[30]

When Thomas Roe returned from the Mughal court, he brought two
antelopes and 'a strange and beautiful kind of red deer' with him, which he
presented to the king at Hampton Court.[31] In 1631, Captain Weddell
brought a leopard for Charles I and a cage of birds for Henrietta Maria.

After the Restoration, orders were sent to Surat and Madras to procure rare beasts and birds for presentation to Charles II. In November 1661, the president and council at Madras reported the dispatch of 'two great and one small antelope, two pelicans, and two noorees or Maccasser parrots'. When Robert Master, chief of the factory at Karwar (on the Malabar Coast) died on Christmas Day 1665, it was reported to Surat that his effects included 'two elks, a speckled deer, and an antelope', some of which had been collected 'to be set ashore to breed at St Helena' and the rest for presentation to the king. The agent and council at Madras also shipped back three does and a buck to England in 1665. When the buck saw the verdant valleys of St Helena, he made a bid for liberty, leaping overboard, and swimming to the shore where he disappeared into the thickets. Evidently, however, many animals did make it to Britain because, on 22 October 1684, John Evelyn noted in his diary that he had gone with Sir William Godolphin to see 'the rhinoceros or unicorn, being the first that, I suppose, was ever brought into England. She belong'd to some East India merchants, and was sold (as I remember) for above £2000.'[32] In 1686, a twopence admission charge was levied for inspection of the creature (fig. 33). Barlow sketched the rhinoceros. He also remarked that, when they were getting ready to leave Surat, they took two or three spotted deer on board 'to carry as a present to the King from the President of the Company at Surat, some of them living and some of them dying, and when we came to Blackwall the keeper of St James' Park came on board for them'.[33]

The impact of East India Company trade on European societies was perhaps most clearly visible in the volume and increasingly wide range of consumer goods brought back to Europe. However, creatures such as the rhinoceros, drawn by Barlow and described by Evelyn, symbolise a heightened awareness of Asia brought about as a direct result of the maritime links between Europe and Asia.

fig. 33
Rhinoceros, by Edward Barlow, 17th century
This rhinoceros, illustrated here by Edward Barlow in his journal, was brought back from India and sold in London for over £2,000 in the 1680s.
[JOD/4/109, detail]

A key objective of early European voyages to the East Indies was to establish cordial relations with local rulers as a basis for future trade. The ability to trade, to establish factories and to carry out business successfully were all dependent on the permission of, and partnership with, indigenous people at all levels. For most of its history the Company operated under the sufferance of local Asian rulers, and it depended on Indian merchants or 'banians' to supply their ships with goods. For example, Lawrence Femell was instructed always to remember 'the honour of our king and country, and the reputations of our negotiators in those parts'. He was to take care to deliver letters 'with that honour which may be well fitting so great a monarch'. And special care was to be taken to uphold 'the honour of our king and the reputation of our trafficke'. Femell played his part well. Nicholas Downton reported that, at the end of October 1610 at Tamarin, Femell went ashore 'handsomely attended with a present (consisting of a fair gilt cup of ten ounces, a sword blade, and three yards of stammel broad cloth) for the King, who surrounded by the principal of his countrymen, the Arabs, received him at the waterside, and having accepted the General's presents, promised to supply water free and whatever else he could'.[34]

In search of spices, the first English fleet put in at Aceh intent on delivering letters of friendship from Queen Elizabeth to the sultan. James Lancaster had been provided with 'two fair, costly looking-glasses, a silver basin and ewer, two standing cups, four silver cups, and other things of less value' to present as gifts to the local rulers. At Aceh, he 'proceeded to deliver him [the sultan] his present, which was a basin of silver, with a fountain in the midst of it, weighing two hundred and five ounces, a great standing cup of silver, a rich looking glass, and a head-piece with a plume of feathers, a case of very fair daggers, a rich wrought embroidered belt to hang a sword in, and a fan of feathers'.[35] This initial contact was quickly followed by the dispatch of diplomatic missions to courts throughout the Indian Ocean region. Foremost among these was that of the Mughal emperor, Jahángír ('Conqueror of the World').

When he arrived in India, William Hawkins was told that he needed permission to trade from the emperor. Hawkins delivered letters from King James to Jahángír when he arrived at Agra in 1609. The emperor was impressed by Hawkins's ability to speak Persian and by his drinking capacity: so much so that he found him a Christian Armenian wife. The idea of maintaining a permanent ambassador at the Mughal court was mooted by Thomas Aldworth. In November 1613, he claimed that this was the only way of having the Company's affairs taken seriously, vis-à-vis their rivals, the Dutch and Portuguese: 'Their [sic] might be a sufficient man sent in your first ships that may be Resident in Agra with the King, and such a one whose person may breed regard, for they here look much after great men.'[36] Back in London, the first governor of the Company, Sir Thomas Smythe, recognised that in order for the commercial relationship with India to develop and thrive they needed 'one of extraordinary parts to reside at Agra to prevent any plots that may be wrought by the Jesuits to circumvent our trade'.[37]

The English victory over the Portuguese at Surat persuaded Jahángír to grant the East India Company permission to establish a trading factory in India. Sir Thomas Roe was employed to represent King James at the Mughal court. Following nearly eight months at sea, Roe's ship anchored at Swally Roads, off Surat. When he eventually reached Jahángír's court, at Ajmer, over four hundred miles north-northeast of Surat, Roe's first impressions of the emperor were favourable. He found Jahángír 'very affable, and of a cheerful countenance, without pride … full of gentle conversation'. The two men became well disposed towards each other: 'I always saw a free and noble jollity [in Jahángír] and … in his conversation a man that lives humanely with men'. Jahángír enjoyed entertaining and feasting, even if it meant that he was liable to suffer from drowsiness brought on by 'the fumes of Bacchus'.[38]

The ritual of present-giving and the maintenance of suitable appearances were crucial parts of diplomatic protocol in Asia. Femell was instructed to deliver 'some honourable present' to 'the Great Mogul and to some of the chief officers of the court'.[39] As many previous European travellers could testify, gift-giving was an essential element in ensuring the success of diplomatic encounters. No serious progress towards trading concessions could be made without creating the correct impression. The 13th-century text, *Adab-u'l-Harb*, specified appropriate types of gifts for diplomatic exchange in south Asia. These included the Qur'an and commentaries on it, slaves, textiles, animals, animal trappings, arms and armour, precious materials and 'China vessels'. Elsewhere in Asia, Chinese and Japanese rulers were no less exacting in the importance they attached to presenting gifts, as illustrated by their meticulous recording of the objects offered by various European embassies.

The consequences of failing to meet the exacting standards of protocol could be serious. The Spanish ambassador, according to Roe, was refused an audience because his gifts were not up to the standard expected by Jahángír. Presents were the recognised medium for establishing credentials and obtaining privileges, and much competition existed between Europeans as to who might offer the most beautiful and expensive objects. When he first met Roe in 1616, Jahángír was intrigued as to 'what kind of curiosities' he might expect from England. The ambassador assured him that they would include 'excellent artifices in painting, carving, cutting, enamelling, figures in brass, copper, or stone, rich embroideries, stuffs of gold and silver'.[40] Jahángír was delighted with the principal offering brought by Roe: an English coach, of which the emperor made two replicas. The Company's annual fleet continued to bring new curiosities each year, such as pictures, embroideries, swords, hats, mastiffs and liquor.

Yet, gift-giving was only one among an array of conventions that Europeans needed to master in order to ensure success in their commercial endeavours. The manner of greeting Asian rulers was a difficult issue. Many European ambassadors bristled at the thought of prostrating themselves before foreign potentates – an act of abasement not required of them even by their own sovereigns. Europeans tried to uphold the dignity of their own king through ostentatious display. Even before treading on Indian soil, European embassies had to present a dignified and regal appearance. The Company ships from which Roe was about to disembark all wore their red waistcloths and their ensigns, flags, pennants and streamers; the ambassadorial party was rowed ashore in a boat preceded by trumpeters and hautbois players, while the fleet saluted with 48 guns. When Roe eventually landed, a guard of 80 seamen armed with pikes and muskets saluted with volleys of shot. While on shore, Roe insisted that his retinue preserve European manners and etiquette at all times. His dining room was furnished with European tables and chairs, while the food was served on silver platters. Roe marked his tents with the flag of St George, and members of his household had to wear European-style clothes. All of them, with the sole exception of the chaplain, wore Roe's livery in public: a red taffeta cloak trimmed with green. Given the tortuous rules of protocol, perhaps it was little wonder that Roe eventually tired of such suffocating strictures. After three years at the Mughal court, experiencing 'the pride and falsehood of these people', Roe was convinced that they 'attended only advantage and were governed by private interest and appetite'.[41]

As the first ambassador to represent the East India Company in India, Roe recognised the difficulty of maintaining a purely trading relationship with Asia. But he noted presciently that 'a war and traffique [i.e. trade] are incompatible'. These irreconcilable impulses had cost the Portuguese and the Dutch, and he warned the East India Company not to go down the same route: 'Let this be received as a rule that if you will [seek] Profit, seek it at sea, and in quiet trade; for without controversy it is an error to effect garrisons and land wars in India.'[42]

One of the most historic results of Roe's embassy was the production of the first English map of India. He had used his time there to compile a list of the kingdoms and provinces of the Mughal Empire, together with the principal rivers and cities. Roe's correspondent, Lord Carew, was alive to the legacy of this endeavour: 'Be careful to make the map of the Mogul's territory as you have intended; it will be a work worthy of yourself and adorn your travel and judgement, and leave to the world a lasting memory when you are dust.' Roe's only conspicuous public memorial is the large mural by Sir William Rothenstein in St Stephen's Hall, Westminster, unveiled in 1927. It was to form part of a scheme epitomising the history of Britain from Alfred the Great to the Anglo-Scottish Act of Union, and depicts Roe's presentation of his credentials to the Mughal emperor. The caption records that Roe 'succeeds by his courtesy and firmness at the court of Ajmir, in laying the foundations of British influence in India, 1614'.[43]

In contrast to the relative success of Roe in negotiating the diplomatic minefields of Asia, the experiences of Robert Knox (fig. 34) illustrate what could happen when there was a breakdown in diplomatic understanding and etiquette. When his ship arrived at Ceylon during an East India Company trading voyage, his father (the captain) made the grave mistake of not sending a letter explaining his presence there along with the customary gifts to the king in order to secure his protection. Knox believed that this lapse in courtesy was the 'main reason of our Surprize', and led to his spending 19 years in captivity. Knox tells us that the King of Kandy, Raja Singha II (reigned 1634/35–1686/87), looked upon himself 'as a great Monarch, as he is indeed, [and] requires to be treated with sutable [sic] State'.[44]

Knox was born in February 1641 at Tower Hill, London. His father was a ship's captain who operated profitably between England and the Levant. In a pattern followed by many others, Knox senior moved into working for the East India Company. In 1655, father and son sailed together in the *Anne* on their first voyage to India. They sailed again from England on 21 January 1658, bound for the Coromandel Coast and Persia. On their way home, after trading for over a year in Bengal, Fort St George and Aceh, their ship was dismasted in a storm at Masulipatam and Captain Knox took her to Kottiar Bay, Ceylon, to fit a new mainmast and to engage in whatever trade was possible. At this time, Raja Singha II had become increasingly wary of the activities of Europeans in his country. In April 1660, after 20 days in port, a royal official came from the court at Kandy to investigate the activities of the English. Fourteen of the crew, including Knox and his father, went ashore where they were promptly taken captive by the king's troops. While the ship and the rest of the crew escaped unscathed, these men were put into open detention in villages, and given food and shelter. Collecting Europeans seems to have been something of a habit with Raja Singha – it is estimated that between five hundred and one thousand captives were living in Kandian villages during his reign. They were rarely mistreated; in fact, these members of what was in effect a European menagerie were a privileged group enjoying royal protection. Knox's father died of malaria within a year. But, despite his ostensible captivity, Knox was able to move around Ceylon, establishing himself as a farmer, moneylender and pedlar. During his 19 years on the

island, he learned the language and adopted local dress and customs, ultimately making his getaway easier. Eventually, he escaped to the Dutch fort at Aripu in 1679. Shortly afterwards, Knox left Bantam in Java for London, where he arrived in September 1680.

During the voyage to England, Knox wrote the manuscript of what became *An Historical Relation of Ceylon*. The book was printed by the Royal Society's printer Richard Chiswell in August 1681 and financed by subscribers from the East India Company. It was widely read and made him famous; it was translated into German, Dutch and French during Knox's lifetime. The book influenced the work of contemporaries such as Daniel Defoe in *Robinson Crusoe* (1719), particularly in Knox's acute observation of details, display of practical self-sufficiency, and strength of character. Nevertheless, Knox's account of his experiences was also useful in providing insights into how to work with Asian people. The ongoing diplomatic drive would continue well into the 18th century.

18TH-CENTURY TRAVELLERS AND AMBASSADORS

In the 18th century, as the volume of East India Company trade expanded, British travellers went to Asia in ever-greater numbers. The heightened interest in travel literature in Europe – second only to novels in numbers sold – gave inspiration to many people to record their impressions in print. Again, appearances made an immediate impression. When Commodore George Anson of the Royal Navy arrived at Canton on his circumnavigation of the globe in the 1740s, he was granted an audience with the Chinese viceroy there. Nothing was spared in creating a spectacle:

As soon as [Anson] entered the outer gate of the city, he found a guard of two hundred soldiers drawn up ready to attend him; these conducted him to the great parade before the Emperor's palace, where the viceroy then resided. In this parade, a body of troops, to the number of ten thousand, were drawn up under arms, and made a very fine appearance, being all of them cloathed [*sic*] for the ceremony.[45]

Unlike many earlier accounts, which detailed the wonders of Chinese civilisation, Anson was critical of the country. This marked a shift in European understanding and expectations of China as the century progressed.

This miniature garden (fig.35) is said to have been brought back from China by Anson. The peach tree is made of coral and the pine tree of carved wood and ivory. Other materials used, such as mother-of-pearl, ivory, malachite and rose quartz, are all symbols of longevity. Nevertheless, if this was brought back by Anson, the party was only mildly impressed by the Chinese manufactures and craftsmen:

fig. 34
Captain Robert Knox of the East India Company, by P. Trampon, 1711
In this portrait, the pistols, quadrant and miniature anchor hanging on the wall refer to Knox's adventures in Asia. His left hand rests on a sheet of paper, bearing the title 'Memoires of my owne life 1708' – an allusion to Knox's best-selling account of his time in Ceylon.

[BHC2825]

fig. 35
Miniature garden, 18th century
Travellers brought back items like this as keepsakes from China in the 18th and 19th centuries. Incorporating symbols of long life and good luck, these objects also advertised Chinese craftsmanship to Europeans.

[OBJ0568]

That the Chinese are a very ingenious and industrious people, is sufficiently evinced, from the great number of curious manufactures which are established amongst them, and which are eagerly sought for by the most distant nations; but though skill in the handicraft arts seems to be the most important qualification of this people, yet their talents therein are but of a second rate kind; for they are much outdone by the Japanese.[46]

William Alexander, an artist (with the official position of 'draughtsman') who accompanied Lord Macartney's diplomatic mission to China later in the century, also remarked on the nature of Chinese goods made specifically for foreigners:

All the shops here are well stocked with goods for sale such as porcelain, japanned wares, cloths & fans, articles of ivory, mother of pearl &c., &c., specimens of which are exposed in front. The various articles are well-suited to the taste of their customers, a traveller being easily induced to expend a considerable sum in purchasing their knick knacks.[47]

fig.36
Shipping in the Pearl River off Honam Island, **Chinese school**, *c.*1840
This image of the bustling seaways around Canton was painted by a Chinese artist, probably for sale to Europeans. It is one of a pair. This depicts a view across the Pearl River, seen from the European factories. The other shows the waterfront at Canton. By the middle of the 18th century, Canton was the only place in China where Europeans were permitted to trade.

[BHC1786]

The carpenter on HMS *Alceste*, a ship that was wrecked in the Java Sea in 1817, bemoaned the loss of the Chinese goods he was bringing back to Britain. His belongings included a 'chest of the best tea, three rolls of silk, three boxes of china, three boxes of sugar, one box of China fans, twenty-four bottles of India soy, three China looking glasses'.[48]

Even in this period, the East India Company still relied on embassies to smooth the path of commerce (fig. 36). The rapid growth of trade with China alerted the Company and the British government to the need for making favourable agreements with the Chinese emperor. Here again, the British were trailing in the wake of the Dutch, Spanish and Portuguese in terms of trading with the region, and it was not until 1637 that a flotilla of ships under John Weddell opened up direct communications with China. Nevertheless, East India Company trade quickly caught up, mainly due to the rise of tea-drinking in Britain. From the first direct consignment of Chinese goods in 1689 to the 1760s, there was a fourfold increase in

Company shipments. To that end, the British government decided to send an embassy to China under the command of George, Lord Macartney in 1792. In an indication of the growing importance of this trade to Europeans, this was only one of numerous European missions to China before 1800. With his previous diplomatic and administrative experience, Macartney was considered to be the best qualified to undertake the task. He certainly entertained a more sanguine and optimistic view of the Chinese than Anson, if verses apparently written in the 1780s are anything to go by:

> Whether I visit China's happy coast
> Climb her fam'd wall, arts yet unrivalled boast
> With wonder gaze on her shores and floods
> Her cities, plains, her mountains rocks and woods.
> Pass the north bounds and Tartar wilds explore
> By ventrous Britons never trod before.[49]

As ever, there was a complex protocol to go through to ensure the success of the mission. Much discussion took place over whether or not Macartney would be asked to perform the traditional *koutou* ceremony, which included prostrating oneself in front of the emperor (the *koutou* involved

fig. 37
Lord Macartney's First Meeting with Qian'long, by William Alexander, 1793
This image shows Lord Macartney's meeting with the Chinese emperor, Qian'long. The boy on the right is the 11-year-old George Thomas Staunton, who impressed the emperor with his spoken Chinese.

[British Library]

three kneelings and nine knockings of the head on the ground) (fig. 37). Again, the choosing and giving of gifts was important. Sending the correct gifts in order to impress, engage curiosity and provide ways to foster future trade connections was crucial. A full list of the objects sent from Britain, together with their valuations, is preserved in the British Library.[50] Macartney eventually left with nearly £18,000 worth of presents, packed in 600 packages, which took some 90 wagons, 40 barrows, 200 horses and 3,000 'coolies' (hired porters) to carry to Peking. All of this effort was intended to assist Macartney who had been instructed by the Company to curry favour with the Chinese in a bid to increase 'the sale of our manufactured articles and of the products of our territories in India'.[51] Objects such as decorative telescopes (fig. 38) were presented to the Chinese emperor by various European embassies. Macartney hoped to impress the Qing court with British scientific technology and to establish the equality of the Chinese emperor and the British king, George III. This mission was unusually well endowed with all manner of scientific instruments. Objects made by people such as Josiah Wedgwood, Matthew Boulton and William Herschel were sent out. As well as being an embassy of information gathering, this was also a trade mission to promote British inventions and manufactures aboard. While the products of Western technology, such as mirrors, lenses, telescopes, clocks and watches were frequently given as gifts from the 17th century onwards, Macartney's embassy took this to new levels.

In an appropriate gesture of the co-operation involved in organising such an expedition, the ambassador was to travel in a naval vessel, HMS *Lion*, while the gifts and part of his retinue travelled in the *Hindostan*, one of the newest and largest ships in the East India Company's fleet. In total, Macartney's retinue consisted of 94 people. Among these were interpreters, scientists ('natural philosophers'), draughtsmen, army officers and five German musicians. Many of those who travelled made copious notes and sketches of what they saw. Macartney was reminded in his official instructions that voyages 'at the public expense in the pursuit of knowledge and for the discovery and observation of distant countries and manners' were one of the glories of George III's reign.[52] As a result, the embassy produced significant volumes of written and visual material. One of those best placed to make such records was William Alexander. Many of Alexander's sketches were used to illustrate later published accounts of the embassy, such as Sir George Staunton's in 1794 and Sir John Barrow's *Travels in China*, published

fig. 38
Decorative telescope, made by Fraser and Son, late 18th century
Scientific instruments and objects such as this telescope were presented to the Chinese by various European embassies. In their pursuit of trading concessions, Europeans tried to impress their hosts with gifts.
[NAV1579]

in 1804. Local Chinese people and scenes were a favourite, such as this view of a 'pleasure junk' (fig.39).

The embassy was to be received in Chengde, a summer retreat north of the Great Wall. Macartney and his suite disembarked from their anchorage and were taken up the river towards Peking in Chinese junks: 'The river here appeared to be as broad as the Thames at Gravesend. Great numbers of houses on each side, built of mud and thatched ... and inhabited by such swarms of people as far exceeded my most extravagant ideas even of Chinese population.' When he arrived at court, however,

fig.39
A Pleasure Junk,
by William Alexander, 1793
William Alexander was the 'draughtsman' on Lord Macartney's diplomatic mission to China in the 1790s. As well as documenting official scenes, he also produced images of everyday life that he saw on his travels, such as this river scene.

[PAD8573]

Macartney was impressed by the 'calm dignity, that sober pomp of Asiatic greatness, which European refinements have not attained'.[53] Nevertheless, difficulties in communications persisted. Macartney noted that 'the Chinese character seems at present inexplicable', while the Chinese frequently found these 'western ocean barbarians' to be 'unfathomable'.[54] Although commercial links had existed between the countries for some time, Britain was relatively little known to the Chinese in the 18th century. There was no single work dealing specifically with Britain published in China (in contrast to the many published about China in Britain). A compilation of 1786 did include a single entry for England (rather than Britain), pointing out that it had one colony and that some of its products, such as clocks and other scientific instruments, were 'incomparably ingenious'.[55]

The Qing court's record of Macartney's embassy provides a fascinating insight into how the Chinese perceived Europeans at this time. A special poem was written to commemorate the visit, which appears in the *Veritable Records of the Qianlong Emperor's Reign* and on a textile hanging, now in the collection of the National Maritime Museum. The *K'o-ssu* tapestry (fig.40) supposedly depicts the arrival of a planetarium and celestial globe at the Summer Palace in September 1793. The artist has not depicted the scene from personal observation because the Europeans are shown in 16th-century dress and the two instruments depicted were already part of the equipment of the Jesuit Observatory in Peking from the 1670s. The poem, which appears in the top right-hand corner of the tapestry, does not present a particularly flattering view of the British. It illustrates how much divergence there could be between European ideas and the reality of the impression they made on the Chinese court:

> For many years the Portuguese have come, presenting gifts
> Now the English have arrived in all sincerity
> Their journey is akin to that of the legendary travellers Shu Hai and Heng Zhang
> The fame of our august ancestors has extended across the vast ocean.
> While they appear ordinary, their hearts are good and true
> Yet their gifts are not precious, but curiosities, whose subtleties have been exaggerated
> Still in cherishing men from afar, no matter how meagre their offerings,
> We treat them with generosity.[56]

Ultimately, the embassy was an expensive and abject failure. Indeed, it marked the beginning of a period of increasingly strained relations between the British and Qing Empires. The emperor received the selected presents as tributes from a subordinate power rather than as gifts from an equal. At the end of the mission, Macartney was pessimistic about the chances of dealing with the Chinese: 'They are a people not to be treated with as civilised

fig.40
K'o-ssu silk tapestry, 18th century
This tapestry purportedly depicts the arrival of scientific instruments at the Chinese emperor's Summer Palace. While both they and the clothing worn by the Europeans were out of date by the time of Macartney's embassy, the sentiments expressed in the poem in the top right-hand corner matched the contemporary Chinese view of official European visitors.

[TXT0107]

European nations', and he described the government as 'the tyranny of a handful of Tartars over more than three hundred millions of Chinese'.[57] He also remarked on the growing rivalry between Britain (and Europe) and China, remarking that 'a few frigates could in a few weeks destroy all their coastal navigation and intercourse'.[58]

Macartney was not the last British ambassador to be rebuffed by the Chinese. Notwithstanding his recognition of the importance of impressing the Chinese, Lord Amherst arrived back at Canton on 1 January 1817 with the news that 'the Emperor of China would not receive him'. When he had left the ship, Amherst and his suite 'were attended by all the captains in the squadron and we fired a royal salute and made the yards and gave him three thundering cheers'. His lordship was so pleased with this rousing send-off that he 'released all the prisoners and "awarded" each man a gallon of strong beer'. While Amherst was failing to make progress at Peking, the captain of the *Alceste* was at 'Lieu Cheu', where he gave the locals 'several handsome presents and showed them great respect and honour'. This was followed by the hosting of a grand banquet where 'we dressed our ship in colours, the Royal Standard at the main'. The Chinese made 'a good tuck out of the port wine till their officers [were as] sore as a salamander in honour of our good old King'.[59]

The response of a select committee of the East India Company at Canton to the rebuttal of Amherst's embassy shows a rising awareness of the thorny issues of dignity and status involved. The perceived degradation and disgrace brought about by consenting to partake in the *koutou* ceremony would have 'fatally shaken the confidence which we have with considerable success established at Canton, in the firm adherence to the principle which distinguishes the British character'. Despite its commercial pretensions, it took a long time for Britain to break into the Chinese trading system – as late as 1828, there were only 25 people on the Company's staff at Canton. There was a dawning recognition that one needed to study cultures according to their own values. As Macartney wrote, 'nothing could be more fallacious than to judge of China by any European standard' (fig. 41).[60]

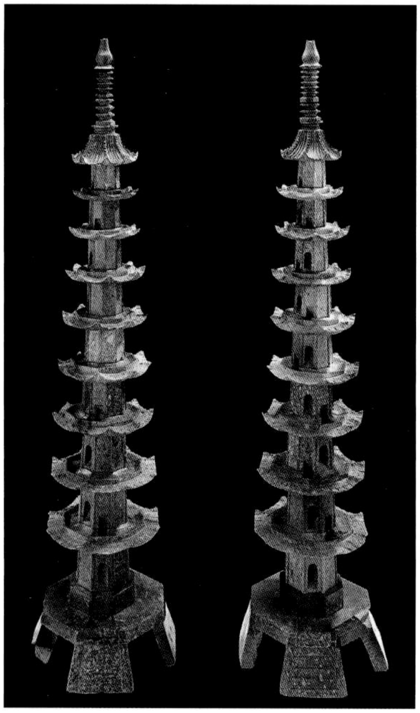

CONCLUSION

William Daniell's *The Watering Place at Anjer Point* (fig. 42) shows HMS *Lion* carrying Macartney back from his failed mission. The convoy included the artist and his uncle, Thomas Daniell, aboard the *Exeter* as they returned to Europe after spending nearly a decade in Asia. The location – the Straits of Sunda – was a well-known convoy rendezvous and watering point on the

fig. 41
Soapstone pagodas, 19th century
This pair of decorative soapstone pagodas was brought back from China in the late 19th century. For many Europeans they symbolised China and its architecture. Sir William Chambers built a 163-foot high pagoda for King George III near Kew in 1762.

[REL0707]

western tip of the island of Java. In his depiction of the scene, with its coastal craft, watering places and indigenous people, Daniell captures the kinds of impressions that were recorded by Europeans as they travelled and traded in Asia.

The painting was later displayed at the Royal Academy, highlighting how knowledge and information about trading and diplomacy with Asians was conveyed to the public back in Europe. Through published accounts, prints and paintings such as this one, the fabulous trading world of Asia that the East India Company had opened up was, quite literally, brought home to Europeans. These encounters seem to mark, in Edmund Burke's evocative phrase, the unrolling of 'the Great Map of Mankind'.[61]

fig. 42
The Watering Place at Anjer Point in the Island of Java, by **William Daniell,** 1794
Daniell's painting depicts a convoy rendezvous in the Straits of Sunda, on the western tip of Java. Although it shows a homeward-bound China fleet in 1793, the painting was exhibited at the Royal Academy in 1836.

[BHC1842]

3

The most illustrious and most flourishing commercial organisation that ever existed

The East India Company's seaborne empire,

1709–1833

H. V. BOWEN

fig. 43
Plate, c.1824
This porcelain plate bears the
Company's Latin motto: 'Auspicio
Regis et Senatus Angliæ' ('By the
Command of the King and
Parliament of England').

[AAA5742]

The development of the East India Company during the first hundred years of its existence was characterised by hesitancy and uncertainty. The Company had built up a regular and often profitable trade with Asia but, under constant threat from rivals and critics, its domestic position was seldom secure. Indeed, at the very end of the 17th century, a serious challenger emerged in the form of a 'new' East India Company, which received a charter from William III in return for a loan of £2 million. This new Company was well resourced and had powerful allies, and it was only after an extended period of political manoeuvring and negotiation that a merger of the two companies was effected and the United Company of Merchants Trading into the East Indies came into being in 1709 (fig. 43). This heralded a period of domestic stability and the Company was then able greatly to strengthen its position on a number of fronts. Trade increased and diversified, notably through greater levels of exchange with China; the Company, together with the Bank of England, became a key financial ally of the British state; and, most important of all, during the second half of the 18th century an extended territorial empire was established in India.

Some of the changes that affected the Company during the 18th century were gradual and almost imperceptible; others, such as the seizure of power in Bengal by Robert Clive in 1757, were sudden and dramatic. Indeed, Clive's actions were held by many to represent a political 'revolution' that had a profound impact not only on the society and economy of Bengal but also the Company itself. While the East India Companies of the Dutch and French fell by the wayside during the second half of the 18th century, the overall effect of these various changes was to transform the status and standing of the British Company. Such was the transformation that in 1805 the political economist David Macpherson described it as being 'the most illustrious and most flourishing commercial organisation that ever existed in any age or country'.[1] But contemporaries also noted that the Company's whole *raison d'être* had been altered fundamentally by the acquisition of territory in India. It now governed millions of people, administered justice and possessed a large army. Following the grant of the *diwani* of Bengal, Bihar and Orissa from the Mughal emperor Shah Alam II in 1765, the Company collected very considerable tax revenues that were used to fund further military and commercial expansion (fig. 44). As early as 1772, one anonymous writer was able to look back over the recent history of the Company and suggest:

[It] had risen from very slender beginnings, to a state of the highest importance; their concerns, simple at first, are grown extremely complex, and are immensely extended. They are no longer mere traders, and confined in their privileges; they are sovereigns over fertile and populous territories.[2]

This was indeed the case and, as territorial expansion continued apace into the 19th century, a Company 'state' was created in India, which meant that Bombay, Calcutta and Madras became seats of British imperial government as well as trading centres.

Many in Britain were deeply uneasy about the fact that the East India Company had become a sovereign as well as a trader, and their concerns increased as reports of corruption and misrule began to find their way back to Britain during the 1760s. Proceedings against leading figures such as Robert Clive and Warren Hastings, together with widespread condemnation of the ill-gotten gains of fabulously wealthy returned Company servants

fig. 44
Shah Alam Conveying the Grant of the Diwani to Lord Clive, August 1765, **by Benjamin West, 1818**
As a result of military successes in Bengal, the Company acquired from Shah Alam, the Mughal emperor, the right to collect taxes there. This additional revenue funded further military and commercial expansion in India.
[British Library]

fig. 45
John Robarts Esqr., Chairman of the East India Company, after George Dance, *c.1810*
The Company was governed by the Court of Directors in London. Chairmanship of the Court was one of the most powerful and influential positions in the City of London.

[PAD3177]

known as 'nabobs', served only to heighten public suspicion of the Company. A series of financial and political crises meant that government intervention was necessary to impose regulation and reform upon East Indian affairs. Lord North's Regulating Act of 1773, Pitt the Younger's India Act of 1784, and various Charter Acts all sought to bring the Company under the control and supervision of the state. This meant that, as far as the empire in India was concerned, the Company became a governing agency of the British crown while continuing to act as an independent trading company. Its home bureaucracy evolved to accommodate the administration of empire as well as trade, and chairmen of the Company such as Sir George Colebrooke, Charles Grant, David Scott and John Robarts (fig. 45) were regarded as being among the most powerful men of the day. As Joseph Hume put it, such men acted as 'the ministers of a state, or as the monarchs of an empire, greater in extent and population, if he excepted China, than any other in the world'.[3]

Yet, at the same time, changing economic attitudes shaped by the writings of Adam Smith and other critics of restrictive trading practices undermined the Company's position by increasingly calling into question the need for continuing trade monopolies. In particular, the Company came under considerable and sustained pressure from provincial merchants and manufacturers in Britain who desired free and open access to markets in Asia. Despite a determined rearguard action in defence of its privileges, the Company gradually lost ground to the free traders, who were able to persuade ministers that a monopolistic East India trade was no longer operating in the best interests of British industry and government finance. Restrictions on trade with India were partially lifted in 1793, and then trade with the subcontinent was thrown fully open to private traders in 1813. British trade with China remained the preserve of the Company for another 20 years, until the Charter Act of 1833 brought an end to over 230 years of continuous maritime trading activity. Yet, even then, such was the profound nature of the changes that had affected the Company since the middle of the 18th century that it survived for a further 25 years, not as a trading company but as the ruler of British India.

It was against a general background provided by this often-uncomfortable transition from trade to empire that the East India Company continued to develop as a maritime trading organisation. From the 1750s in particular, the consequences arising from territorial expansion in India were felt, in small ways as well as large, across all areas of the Company's activities, and this chapter explores some of the ways in which change manifested itself at home, abroad and at sea.

EAST INDIA HOUSE: THE DOMESTIC ARCHITECTURE OF TRADE AND EMPIRE

To casual observers in London, the change in status experienced by the East India Company was perhaps most evident in the significant alterations that were made to its headquarters, East India House, or the 'India House' as it was increasingly known during the late 18th century.[4] During the early years of its fragile existence, the Company had leased several modest sites in the City of London that acted in turn as the headquarters for the fledgling trading corporation. A permanent home for the Company was only established in 1647, when a lease was taken out on a building owned by Lord Craven in Leadenhall Street. 'Craven House', as it was originally known, was located on a site a quarter of a mile to the east of the City of London. Standing next to the busy Leadenhall Market, at the junction of Lime Street and Leadenhall Street, the building proved to be convenient for stockholders and officials alike, being close to the capital's financial institutions, the River Thames and the Company's several warehouses. The United Company eventually purchased the site in 1710, and the headquarters remained at this location until the end of the Company's days in 1858.

The Leadenhall Street site was progressively redeveloped during the course of the 18th century, a process which in many ways reflected the advancement of the Company's commercial and political fortunes. The original, cramped, wooden house had become rather dilapidated by the 1720s, and between 1726 and 1729 it was replaced by a much grander Palladian-style building designed by the architect Theodore Jacobsen. This four-storey brick building had a narrow frontage, but it extended far back from the street. Additional spaces and new offices were created in 1754 when an extension designed by William Jones was completed following the demolition of an adjacent property, which had been purchased by the Company in 1717. Even so, within a couple of decades it was felt in some quarters that the Company's ambition and success in India had not been matched by the further development of its headquarters. As James Northouck put it in 1773: 'It has been remarked that the appearance of the building is nowise suited to the opulence of the Company, whose servants exercise sovereign authority in their Indian territories and live there in a princely state.'[5]

In part motivated by a desire to possess a building whose exterior fully reflected the Company's late-18th-century commercial and imperial status, the directors ordered a full-scale expansion and development of the House during the 1790s (fig. 46). Following the purchase of a number of nearby houses and taverns in Lime Street and Leadenhall Street, this work was carried out between 1796 and 1799 by the masons Pinder and Norris. They

fig. 46
A View of the East-India House, Leadenhall Street, 1802
The East India Company had its headquarters in the City of London. It occupied a series of buildings, each one grander than the last. This impressive edifice reflects the Company's prestige and power.

[PAH2178]

operated under the supervision of two architects: Richard Jupp, the Company surveyor, who died in April 1799, and his successor, Henry Holland. Although the House could only be extended slightly beyond its existing limits, the outward appearance was much improved, a new Sale Room was added, and more effective use was made of existing space through the construction of a central corridor running through the building.

It was intended that the new façade of the building would leave onlookers in little doubt as to the success, wealth and utility of the Company, and Jupp executed his commission with this in mind. The façade that he designed measured 190 feet in length and 60 feet in height, and it was adorned with elaborate symbolic representations of the ways in which the Company was held by contemporaries to define Britain's links with its eastern empire. The centrepiece, placed above six Ionic columns standing in front of the entrance hall, was a pediment decorated by John Bacon and described by an anonymous contemporary observer as containing 'an enriched Grecian frieze, and a much-admired cornice for its commodious projecture'. Here, in Roman dress, was to be found George III 'shielding

Britannia and Liberty, at whose feet is Asia pouring out treasures'. To the left of the king was 'Commerce represented by Mercury attended by navigation, triton, horse, [and] elephant, with the Ganges filling the East Angle', while to his right sat 'order attended by religion, industry and integrity, the City Barge, and the Thames fill the West Angle'. Above the pediment stood Britannia, astride a lion with, to the east, Asia upon a camel and, to the west, Europe upon a horse. To the side of East India House that ran along Lime Street a Portland stone front 140 feet in length had been added, into which had been built a 'neat entrance' to the Seaman's Lobby leading to the Pay Office. It was intended that into the 14-foot niche that had been carved out above the 'great window' in the wall would be placed 'the emblematical figure of two sailors with their hands united over a globe shaded by an oak tree'. The building as a whole had been surrounded by a 'pallisade of excellent workmanship', and an early-19th-century Indian visitor to London was certainly impressed by what he saw.[6] Mirza Abu Taleb Khan declared that '[t]he India House is a very extensive and superb building, and contains an immense number of apartments for all the public offices', and he noted that 'including the warehouses [it] is not less than a mile in circumference'.[7]

With many contemporary motifs of seaborne trade and empire on external display to passers-by in Leadenhall Street by the end of the 18th century, East India House offered an outward architectural expression of the values and virtues thought to be embodied by the Company housed within. Such imagery also came to be deployed in the internal decoration of the Company's headquarters and, over time, this reflected the transition from trading corporation to imperial power.[8] During the early part of the 18th century, emphasis was quite naturally placed upon the benefits derived from

fig. 47
The Cape of Good Hope, after Samuel Scott and George Lambert, *c.*1750
This print was based on one of the paintings by Samuel Scott and George Lambert that hung in the Court Room of East India House in London. The six canvases depicted locations that were strategically and commercially important for the Company.

[PAI0249]

successful maritime commerce. Thus, during the renovation of the late 1720s, the Company's achievements to date were celebrated in lavish style, particularly in the room occupied by the Court of Directors. Here a large marble mantelpiece, designed by the Dutch sculptor Michael Rysbrack and completed in 1730, supported a chimney piece which contained an elaborate bas-relief depicting Britannia receiving the riches of the East. A number of canopies supported by colonnades decorated the walls, with the gilded Company coat of arms standing above the canopy in front of which was placed the chairman's seat. Oil paintings for the Court Room were commissioned from George Lambert and Samuel Scott in 1732, and these depicted the Company's six main trading stations, as well as some of the Indiamen that visited them (fig. 47). Furnishings for the room included large tables and armchairs, all of whose legs were adorned with elaborate carved masks, while mirrors and chandeliers hung from the walls and ceiling.

In the years that followed, the Company continued to adorn the building with minor furnishings, paintings and porcelain plate, and many of these items continued to celebrate the Company's commercial activities

fig. 48
India House. The Sale Room, after **Thomas Rowlandson, 1808**
The business affairs of the Company were directed from London. The Sale Room in India House was one of the most important commercial centres for the British economy.

[PAD1361]

THE EAST INDIA COMPANY'S SEABORNE EMPIRE, 1709–1833

and worth to the nation. But from the 1760s onwards, the internal decoration of East India House also began to reflect the pride that the Company took in its military and political successes on the Indian subcontinent. This trend began in 1760 when the Dutch sculptor Peter Scheemakers was commissioned to produce statues of Lord Clive, Major-General Stringer Lawrence and Sir George Pocock, all of whom had played key roles in the actions which saw the Company assert its supremacy over European and Indian rivals. Scheemakers completed his work in 1764, and the full-length figures dressed in Roman costume were placed in niches, high above the large Sale Room in which auctions of East India goods were conducted and meetings of the stockholders were held (fig. 48). Two further statues of military figures were later placed in other niches. A commission to sculpt a statue of Sir Eyre Coote was executed by Thomas Banks in 1784, and ten years later John Bacon produced a likeness of Lord Cornwallis. By the beginning of the 19th century, these figures would have confirmed to observers that the Company had now evolved into an imperial organisation that was successfully combining commercial and military functions. Any lingering doubts about this would have been dispelled by a visit to the central courtyard of East India House, where two of Tipu Sultan's cannon had been placed following their capture at the siege of Seringapatam in 1799.

THE COMPANY AND THE METROPOLIS

Although East India House came to serve as the administrative headquarters for the Indian empire, it by no means represented the full extent of the Company's presence in Britain. From the 1620s, the Company had maintained an almshouse in Poplar for the benefit of its disabled or impoverished seamen, and a Company chapel had been built nearby in 1654. Warehouses had been built or rented close to East India House, and the Company continued to develop the commercial infrastructure necessary to support the growth of maritime trade. Moreover, during the early years of the 19th century, it also began to establish additional facilities deemed appropriate for a military and imperial power. For example, a formal Company presence was established beyond London in places such as Haileybury, where the East India College was set up, and the Isle of Wight, where there was a military depot.

The most obvious and tangible expressions of late-18th-century Company commercial strength were, however, always to be found in London itself, notably in the form of the warehouses built to store an increasingly large volume of goods imported from India and China. Initially, most Company warehouses were located between East India House and the Legal

fig. 49

The Mast House and Brunswick Dock at Blackwall, by William Daniell, *c.*1803

This painting gives a bird's-eye view of Perry's (later Green's) Brunswick Dock at Blackwall looking down the Thames towards Woolwich. East Indiamen are moored up in lines to the left and centre in the nearer part of the dock, many only partly rigged. The distinctive Blackwall masting house in the foreground, surrounded by piles of timber, fitted many of these ships with their masts.

[BHC1867]

Quays on the River Thames, where goods were unloaded from the hoys that carried cargo from East Indiamen moored in Blackwall Reach. Although warehouses were to be found quite close to East India House, they were scattered somewhat haphazardly in a variety of locations in Billiter Lane, Coopers' Row, Crutched Friars, French Ordinary Court, Haydon Square, Fenchurch Street, Jewry Street and Leadenhall Street. In addition, some spices were stored in the 'Pepper Cellar' at the Royal Exchange, and saltpetre was removed a safe distance to a magazine at Ratcliff Cross.[9] After 1765, however, the need to store greater quantities of bulk commodities, including thousands of chests of tea, led to new warehouses being constructed further afield, most notably in the area north of Leadenhall Street between Bishopsgate and Petticoat Lane. The New Street Warehouse (later known as the Old Bengal Warehouse) was completed between 1768 and 1771 and then, following a marked increase in the Company's import trade, extensive purchases of land in and around Gravel Lane enabled a large integrated complex known as the Cutler Street Warehouses to be built between 1792 and 1800. This building programme had a considerable impact upon the locality, and contemporaries were impressed not only with the size and scale of the buildings but also the sense of order and cleanliness that had been brought to a hitherto dirty and densely populated neighbourhood.

THE EAST INDIA COMPANY'S SEABORNE EMPIRE, 1709–1833

At the same time, the pressures of an expanding trade, together with loss and inconvenience caused by a slow cargo-unloading process on the Thames, combined to prompt the construction of an East India dock complex between 1803 and 1806. The initiative for this development lay in the hands of the newly established East India Dock Company rather than the East India Company itself (fig. 49). This ambitious construction project, which was part of the early-19th-century London dock-building boom, saw the purchase and enlargement of the Brunswick Dock or 'Perry's Dock' at Blackwall, which had long been used to build and service Company ships and had a reputation as 'the most considerable private dock in Europe'.[10] From the new East India Dock imported goods were now transported to the Company's City warehouses in heavily protected caravans.

TRADE AND TRIBUTE

The building of new docks and warehouses in London arose from the Company's urgent need to cope with a rapid expansion of trade that was driven in large part by the acquisition of huge swathes of territory in Bengal (fig. 50). This was because possession of territories and revenues in India led to a swift and fundamental remodelling of the Company's entire trading system. Long-held assumptions and calculations about the conduct of business were readily abandoned during the 1760s, as directors and officials sought ways to transfer new-found riches to Britain in the form of 'tribute'. In part, a remittance of surplus revenues was to be achieved by increased investment in cotton textiles and raw silk for direct export to London (fig. 51). At the same time, Indian commodities known to be in demand in China were shipped to Canton to provide funds for the purchase of greater amounts of tea for shipment to Britain. Indeed, during the late 18th century, the growth of the tea trade went hand in hand with the expansion of empire as the Company developed a form of triangular trade between Britain, India and China. As this happened, straightforward trade for trade's sake was adapted to a new purpose by the Company. This development prompted the Abbé Raynal to comment that '[t]hey are no longer a *commercial* society, they are a *territorial* power who make the most of their revenues by the assistance of a traffic that formerly was their sole existence'.[11]

Within this new trading system there was now much less need for the Company to transfer large amounts of silver to Asia. But woollen cloth and metals such as iron, lead and copper were still shipped directly from London to India and China on the Company's account, and a series of export drives led to some growth of this trade during the last decades of the 18th century. Later, the Company also began cautiously to experiment with the export of

fig. 50
Ten-cash piece, 1808
The arms of the East India Company are visible on one side of this coin; the other side bears an inscription in Persian. As the effective government of large parts of India, the Company collected taxes, struck coins and issued money.
[MEC2729]

fig. 51
Bag seal, c. 1780
Seals like this were folded and clamped around bolts or bales of cloth. The letters 'VEIC', set within a heart shape, represent the mark of the 'United East India Company'.
[ZBA0441]

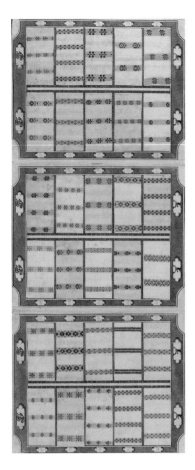

cotton cloth manufactured in Britain, despite concerns that such action would serve only to damage the Indian textile industry (fig. 52). Most significantly, though, intra-Asian or 'country' trade once more became of great importance to the British. For the most part, it was left to private traders and not the Company itself to carry large consignments of raw cotton and, increasingly, opium from India to China.

In seeking to grow its trade in tea, the Company was obliged to conduct its commercial business in China in ways that were very different from those used in India. European traders had been confined to Canton on the Pearl River from 1715 onwards, and the Chinese imperial authorities regulated their presence at the port very tightly indeed. For example, Company ships had to anchor some distance away from Canton at Whampoa, and this meant that loading and unloading East Indiamen was a complex and lengthy process taking weeks on end (fig. 53). In addition, the dozen or so Company merchants (or 'supercargoes') were not permitted to remain in their Canton factory throughout the year, and when the trading season came to an end they had to retire to nearby Macao. Also inconvenient was an organisational arrangement designed to ensure that all foreign trade was conducted with the small group of Chinese merchants known as the Hong Merchants, and a prohibition on inland travel meant that the Company was denied access to first-hand information about internal conditions and markets. Unsurprisingly, perhaps, these circumstances regularly caused considerable friction between the British traders and the Chinese authorities, and matters were made worse when Company merchants or visiting sailors were charged with crimes and misdemeanours (figs 54, 55 and 56).

fig. 52
Fabric pattern book,
Manchester, 1819
Textiles were mass-produced in Britain by the early 1800s, eventually supplanting Indian-made goods. This book contains samples of Manchester cottons for export to India.
[HMN/130]

fig. 53
Whampoa in China,
after William John Huggins, 1835
The Chinese did not permit any European vessels to anchor at Canton. Instead, European and American ships moored at Whampoa, about eight miles down the Pearl River.
[PAI0239]

fig. 54

The Trial of Four British Seamen at Canton: The Scene Outside the Court, **Chinese artist, c.1807**
After an altercation in Canton, which resulted in the death of a man, trade with Company ships was suspended by the Chinese authorities. Four British seamen accused of involvement are depicted arriving at the Chinese Court of Justice. The Chinese figure speaking to the sailors points towards the main courtroom entrance, identified by the red-ribbon swag above the door.

[BHC0580]

fig. 55

The Trial of Four British Seamen at Canton: The Scene Inside the Court, **Chinese artist, c.1807**
Seated on the right of the court are the Hong merchants who controlled trade with Europeans. Facing them are the leading British merchants and officials in Canton. After this trial, one sailor from the East Indiaman *Neptune* was convicted of accidental homicide.

[BHC0581]

fig. 56 *(overleaf)*

A View of the European Factories at Canton, **by William Daniell, c.1790**
The warehouses or 'factories' run by European companies trading at Canton, the contact zone between China and the West, are depicted on the riverfront. Canton is shown as thriving and populous, suggesting the volume of trade conducted there.

[ZBA1291]

fig. 57
Tea chest, 19th century
This lacquered black tea chest is
inlaid with mother-of-pearl. The
gold Chinese characters on the lid
refer to the 'chop', or brand name
of the tea seller.

[AAB0462]

fig. 58
The Charlotte of Chittagong *and
Other Vessels at Anchor in the River
Hoogli,* by Franz Balthazar Solvyns,
1792
Private British and Indian traders
used vessels like this to carry goods
between Asian ports. They were
often built in Indian shipyards. The
artist lived in Calcutta for over ten
years. Here he shows two views of
the *Charlotte,* broadside and stern,
a common convention.

[BHC1100]

Yet, despite all of the operational difficulties and frustrations
experienced at Canton, when the Company's supercargoes were provided
with greater levels of funding from Britain and India after 1765 they were
able to procure ever-greater amounts of tea from the Hong Merchants. The
results were striking, especially after 1784 when, in a bid to defeat large-scale
smuggling from Europe, the government of William Pitt the Younger
slashed the rate of duty on tea imported into Britain. Demand for legal
tea rose very sharply. Whereas during the early 1750s the Company had
imported only around three million pounds of tea every year, by the end of
the century annual imports were somewhere in the region of twenty million
pounds. The Company was still shipping large quantities of cotton textiles
into London from India, together with important commodities such as raw
silk and saltpetre, but there was no denying that within the East India trade
as a whole a swing to China had taken place. In terms of value, this was
demonstrated during the first decade of the 19th century, when two-thirds of
all goods sold by the Company in London had been imported from Canton.
As a parliamentary committee concluded in 1812, in commercial terms China
was now the 'most important branch of the Company's concerns' (fig. 57).[12]

The growth of the Company's import trade was undeniably impressive.
But at no time did official Company trade ever represent the full extent
of the East India trade. Private traders had always sought access to Asian
markets and the business opportunities that were available in the East. A few
of these men were licensed 'free merchants', but most were Company servants
stationed in India, who were well positioned to conduct country trade across
the Indian Ocean (fig. 58). Over time, some of their businesses evolved into

powerful and well-resourced 'agency houses' and this brought new levels of organisation to British private trade through the creation of shipping, insurance and financial services. Benefiting from this process were men such as the appropriately named Money brothers: William, James and Robert (fig. 59). They were able to combine different types of Company service with private trade to such an extent that their family business empire eventually extended from Bombay and Calcutta to Canton.

Other entrepreneurial individuals made the most of opportunities to undertake long-distance private trade between Britain and Asia. The commanders and officers of East Indiamen operated what was known as the 'privilege trade' under licence from the Company, but they also smuggled considerable quantities of goods out of Indian ports and Canton (fig. 60).

fig. 59
The Money Brothers,
by John Francis Rigaud, 1788–92
This portrait shows (from left to right) Robert, William and James Money, three brothers all in Company service. It took several years to complete the painting because the brothers could only sit for the artist when visiting Britain. The finished work was exhibited at the Royal Academy in 1792.
[BHC2866]

Many of these men were known by contemporaries to have made large fortunes from trading on their own account, and as a result the command of an East Indiaman was a highly coveted maritime appointment that could cost up to £5,000 to purchase. Also involved in long-distance private trading activity were interlopers and clandestine traders, who conducted an often high-volume illicit trade between Britain and India via mainland Europe. Their enduring presence meant that at all times there were important flows of commodities which were not under the direct control of the Company, and these added greatly to the overall volume and diversity of the East India trade. The Company restricted itself to a bulk trade in staple commodities such as tea, textiles and raw materials, but more adventurous private traders tended to focus their attention on the fine goods that were in demand with consumers in Britain and elsewhere. As a result, the consignments of East Indian commodities shipped to London through the private trades usually contained an assortment of luxury and semi-luxury items that were destined to find their way into the homes of the middling and upper orders. When the *Wexford* returned to London from Canton in 1812, its cargo contained a vast array of private goods in addition to the tea it carried on the Company's account. An inventory presented details of drawings, pictures, backgammon tables, chess boards, fans, lacquered ware, cane floor mats, screens, toys, sticks for parasols, ornaments, silk clothing and chinaware, as well as a variety of miscellaneous objects.[13] The presence of an abundant quantity of such items on board the *Wexford* illustrates the extent to which the East India trade continued to reshape patterns of consumption in Britain, and how Indian and Chinese goods had been woven firmly into the social fabric of the nation (fig. 61). Not only had cotton and silk textiles remained popular, but tea was now so avidly consumed across all social classes that the Company was obliged by statute to keep a year's supply in reserve in its warehouses. It was commonplace for many well-to-do households to display extensive collections of porcelain, tableware, furnishings, decorations and art work that had been imported from the East (figs 62, 63 and 64).

fig. 60
Chinese snake boat
This is a model of a Chinese snake boat, which was commonly used as a smuggling vessel in the Pearl River Delta around Canton.
[AAE0143]

fig. 61
Embroidered silk waistcoat, 18th century
Fine silks, like this waistcoat, became available as a result of Company trade. But they remained expensive, luxury items that only the wealthiest could afford.
[UNI3643]

fig. 62

Vase, *c.*1800

This large vase, made of glazed stoneware, includes common Chinese symbols and motifs. The silver band on the rim records the vase as having been 'Given by the Queen of Naples to the saviour of Europe, the illustrious Baron Nelson of the Nile, at Palermo in the month of July 1800 AD'.

[AAA4723]

fig. 63
Export porcelain, *c.*1770
These items were made in China for export to Europe. They belonged to Mrs Elizabeth Cook, the wife of the famous explorer, Captain James Cook.

[AAA6192, AAA6193, AAA6194 AND AAA6195]

fig. 64
Ceramics belonging to Lord Nelson, *c.*1802
These items form part of a breakfast service that belonged to Admiral, Lord Nelson. Although they are based on a 'Japan' pattern, they were made in Worcester by Chamberlain's China Factory, which Nelson visited in August 1802. The soaring demand for porcelain items from Asia encouraged British manufacturers to imitate them in design and material.

[AAA4532, AAA4536, AAA4540 AND AAA4544]

fig. 65
Merchantman, *c.*1840
This model of a Blackwall-built
merchantman is constructed at
a scale of 1:48. It represents
a 900-ton ship measuring over
150 feet long. Ships like this brought
huge quantities of tea from China
to supply an increasing demand in
Britain and the rest of the world.

[SLR0847]

The rapid expansion of trade and empire during the second half of the 18th century was reflected in a significant growth of the Company's fleet of East Indiamen. During the 1760s, 25 ships a year were dispatched to Asia, but by the 1800s the number of annual departures had doubled to 50. This meant that, at its peak, the Company had up to 200 ships either at sea or preparing for voyages at any one moment. At the same time, the average size of an East Indiaman increased from between 500 and 750 tons to between 1,000 and 1,200 tons as larger vessels were employed to carry substantial cargoes of tea from Canton to London (fig.65). As in earlier years, these ships had to be heavily armed. The East Indiamen of the mid-18th century carried 26 nine-pounder guns, but some of the later ships employed in the China trade had the capacity to mount up to 56 cannon. This fighting capacity marked out the Company's ships as being very different from ordinary merchant vessels, as was highlighted during engagements when they demonstrated that they were capable of giving as good as they received from enemy warships.

Most of the ships in the Company's large fleet were still hired from private owners, having been constructed on the Thames in the yards of builders such as William Barnard (fig.66), John Perry, Randall & Brent, and the Wells family. But from the mid-1770s, the Company also began to build a small number of its own ships in India. At the Bombay Dockyards, Parsi master-shipbuilders such as Maneckjee Lowjee and Jamsetjee Bomanjee

fig.66
Punch bowl, c.1785
The interior of this Chinese bowl, made specifically for export, is inscribed: 'Success to Mr Barnard's Yard'. The Barnards were a family of shipbuilders who owned yards at Ipswich, Harwich and Deptford. The Chinese artist who painted the scene around the outside would have used European engravings to assist him in depicting the ships in frame. However, the buildings, scenery and river are distinctively Chinese.

[AAA4440]

(fig.67) supervised the construction of large teak-built vessels for use in the China trade, and ships such as the *Scaleby Castle* and the *Charles Grant* were widely admired as being among the finest vessels of their day (fig.68). The teak ships also had service lives that were much longer than the oak vessels built in Britain. Perhaps unsurprisingly, the London owners of East Indiamen were always resolutely opposed to the use of 'India-built' ships in the East India trade, but the Bombay vessels proved their worth when shipbuilding supplies became scarce in Europe during the 1790s at a time when Britain was at war with France. They also proved to be invaluable to the nation at large when, during the crisis year of 1800, Company ships built in India were able to bring large quantities of rice to Britain where a severe food shortage had been caused by a harvest failure.

Managing the Company's fleet was a complex and difficult task, not least because the ships belonged to owners who formed a powerful group known as the 'shipping interest', but the organisation of sailings into 'seasons' brought a sense of order and regularity to maritime affairs. Export cargoes were assembled so that ships could be dispatched to the East between

fig.67
Jamsetjee Bomanjee, **attributed to John Dorman,** *c.*1830
Jamsetjee was a highly skilled shipwright in Bombay. His family were Parsi shipbuilders from Surat. He built ships for the Company, the Royal Navy and private traders. His family, the Wadias, also traded between India and China.

[BHC2803]

November and April, a strict timing for departure that was essential if winds were to be picked up in the South Atlantic and Indian Ocean. And, in theory if not always in practice, voyages were tightly regulated by the general terms of charter-party agreements as well as the detailed sailing instructions issued to commanders. But, of course, voyages to Asia still remained extremely hazardous, and there was always a danger that the Company would lose ships and valuable cargoes to shipwreck, storm, fire and enemy action. Company vessels often completed their voyages as much through good fortune as sound judgement, and it is little wonder that safe arrivals at a destination were always a cause for much celebration (fig. 69). There was plenty that could go wrong on any voyage, and the public were always reminded of this when an East Indiaman was lost at sea.

The events surrounding the wrecking of Indiamen were always reported in great detail in the newspapers, and artists often gave visual expression to these maritime disasters in paintings that were regularly reproduced as prints. The wrecking of the *Grosvenor* off the south-eastern coast of Africa in 1782 was especially compelling because only a handful of the hundred or so

fig. 68
East Indiamen in the China Seas,
by **William John Huggins,** *c.*1820
This large painting depicts several East Indiamen at sea. The artist probably began his working life at sea and served in the East India Company as a steward and assistant purser on board the *Perseverance,* which sailed for Bombay and China in December 1812.

[BHC1157]

fig. 69
Glass tumbler, c.1783
This tumbler carries the legend:
'Success to the Berrington' and
represents the kind of decorative
material produced to commemorate
long-distance trading voyages.

[GGG0455]

survivors came through the terrible ordeal of walking to safety over hundreds of miles of inhospitable terrain. However, it was the wrecking of outward-bound East Indiamen trying to navigate the difficult waters of the English Channel that really captured the public imagination because these events close to home were tragedies that sometimes involved a large loss of life as well as acts of great personal sacrifice. Many contemporaries were especially touched by the wrecking of the *Halsewell* off the Isle of Purbeck in 1786 because it gave rise to a number of works centred on the heroic actions of Commander John Pierce, who was depicted as going down with his ship while holding on to his two young daughters. In a rather different way, the loss of the *Earl of Abergavenny* near Weymouth in 1805 was represented as a human tragedy on a grand scale because 250 of the 452 people on board failed in their desperate attempts to make the short distance from ship to shore as the vessel slowly broke up and sank after running onto the dangerous shoal known as The Shambles. Among those who drowned was the ship's commander, John Wordsworth, the younger brother of the poet, William, who was devastated by his loss, and this has served to invest the whole disaster with an even greater sense of tragedy. Yet for all the trauma and suffering associated with the wrecking of any East Indiaman, it would be wrong to suggest that the Company lost ships on a regular basis. Certainly there were times when losses were heavy, as happened between 1779 and 1783 when 19 vessels fell victim to the weather, fire, human error or enemy action. But across the period as a whole, Company ships had a reasonably good survival rate by contemporary standards. The Company itself calculated that between 1760 and 1796, 1,038 ships sailed for Asia, with only 51 of them failing to return, and this represented an overall loss rate of about one ship in 20, or roughly five per cent (fig. 70).

Of course, there was a need for the Company to respond to the unwelcome prospect of losing its vessels and their valuable cargoes. Although the coppering of hulls was only introduced slowly at the end of the 18th century because of stubborn opposition from cost-conscious owners, significant improvements were made to the construction of East Indiamen (fig. 71). This arose largely from the actions of the Company's Surveyor of Shipping, the indefatigable Gabriel Snodgrass, who insisted on the use of round-headed rudders, thicker floors, flush upper decks, and iron knees and brackets in all ships built for the Company. The strengthening of East Indiamen was intended to prevent the foundering of ships at sea, but it was also recognised that closer attention had to be paid to navigation, which required the production of more accurate charts and maps. This task fell to the Company's first hydrographer, Alexander Dalrymple, who analysed a vast amount of maritime information accumulated by the Company in London

fig.70

The Wreck of the East Indiaman
Dutton *at Plymouth Sound, 26 January
1796,* **by Thomas Luny, 1821**
The *Dutton* was built on the Thames
in 1781 and chartered by the East
India Company. Life aboard an East
Indiaman was precarious, even in
relatively well-known waters. The
ship was wrecked in Plymouth
Sound during a gale in January 1796.

[BHC3298]

fig.71

**Barnacle taken from the hull
of an Indiaman, 19th century**
This barnacle was scraped from the
hull of an East Indiaman.
Thousands of these crustaceans
could colonise a ship, slowing its
progress through the water and
damaging its timbers. Sailing in the
warm waters of the Indian Ocean
made the Company's ships especially
prone to such problems. They
required constant and costly
maintenance.

[AAB0222]

(fig.72). From his exhaustive studies emerged a selection of printed plans and charts that were distributed to all commanders of East Indiamen. This helped later commanders to avoid navigational errors of the type that had seen the *Colebrooke* wrecked when it struck a rock after entering False Bay in South Africa in 1778. Over time, too, a combination of well-built ships and better navigational practice served significantly to reduce many voyage times to the East. During the 1760s, voyages from London to Bengal often took seven or eight months, but in 1829 the *Marquis of Wellington*, which was making its ninth and final sailing to India, completed a non-stop trip to the same destination in the record-breaking time of 81 days.

Underlying changes to the fleet of East Indiamen also occurred because the Company began to use its ships as rather more than trading vessels. In large part this was because the transformation of the Company's status in India required the deployment of greater levels of manpower on the subcontinent, which meant that there was an increase in the number of people that needed to travel between Britain and the subcontinent. As a result, a broader range of passengers was to be found on board East Indiamen, and this served to alter the whole nature of the voyaging experience for all concerned. Whereas ships on the early voyages carried mostly those who were actually needed to sail the vessel, the East Indiamen of the late 18th century often conveyed a significant number of passengers, including women and children as well as 'landsmen'. Company ships routinely served as troop transports as well as trading vessels which meant that, in addition to a crew of between 100 and 130 men, they sometimes had several hundred soldiers on board as well. There were also Company servants and administrators, together with their wives and children, as well as a sprinkling of diplomats, travellers and missionaries. They created a small, tightly packed shipboard community that had to live in close proximity to one another for up to nine months at a time. This was far from easy in difficult conditions at sea, and for most of those on board an East Indiaman, voyages were a tedious, unpleasant and often terrifying experience.

The senior Company officials and dignitaries who travelled on East Indiamen were afforded at least some degree of comfort because they were accommodated in the airy round house or poop and had the privilege of taking meals alongside senior officers at the captain's table (fig.73). Such passengers often ate well, especially during the early part of a voyage when fresh provisions were abundant. In 1792, for example, Thomas Twining was pleasantly surprised to find that shipboard dinners 'exhibited an abundance and variety, which surprised me, consisting of many joints of mutton and pork variously dressed, curries and pillaus, chickens, ducks, and on Sundays turkeys and hams'. 'It was', he said, 'almost inconceivable where so many things could be stowed, and how they could be dressed and served up day after day.'[14]

But most passengers were not so fortunate and instead were allocated a small amount of cabin space on the second deck. These living quarters were extremely basic, as Mrs Mary Sherwood found when she travelled to India on board the overcrowded *Devonshire* in 1805. She wrote:

> Our cabin was just the width of one gun, with room beside for a small table and single chair. Our cot, slung cross-ways over the gun, could not swing, there not being height sufficient…. We were also in constant darkness…. When the pumps were at work, the bilge water ran through this miserable place, this worse than dog kennel, and to finish the horrors of it, it was only separated by a canvas partition from the place in which the soldiers sat, and I believe, slept and dressed.[15]

Conditions were even worse for members of the ship's crew. They were lodged on the lower deck which was especially cramped, dank, airless and uncomfortable. They existed on a diet that was unappetising and unhealthy: bread or biscuit, salted beef and pork, and pease soup, together with foul water, beer, and the grog that was served at noon every day. Little attention was paid to preserving the health of these men and consequently scurvy, fatigue and illness, as well as accidents, all took their toll on the sailors. The logs and journals of East Indiamen routinely recorded the loss of life and burials at sea. Hence, to take just one example, when the *Boddam* sailed to Madras and China between 1790 and 1792, 11 men lost their lives during the course of the voyage.[16] Most were described simply as having 'departed this life', and their bodies were then 'committed to the deep' the following day. But William Harries, carpenter's first mate, and Swain Anderson Burr, seaman, both died after falling from the main yard in separate incidents; and Thomas Langton drowned after he fell into the sea while scraping barnacles from the bends, the timbers which formed the ribs or sides of a ship. On this last occasion, the commander John Jones launched the jolly boat in an attempt to find Langton and 'fish him up' but this rescue action was in vain and the unfortunate seaman could not be saved. Such losses were tragic but commonplace, and the Company's ordinary seamen endured a hard life at sea, often dying with very few possessions to their name (fig. 74).

For passengers not used to travelling by sea, voyages to the East could be unpleasant in the extreme, and many were affected by the sickness that resulted from the ship's pitching and rolling in heavy seas. Even before the *Plassey* had left the Channel on its passage to Madras in 1769, William Hickey 'turned deadly sick'. He was 'obliged to retire to my cot, from whence I scarcely stirred for ten days, during which I was in a very lamentable condition, straining so violently, from having nothing in my stomach to throw up, that I often thought I must, like my mother, die upon the ocean'. In the Bay of Biscay, 'tempestuous weather' combined with

fig. 73

An Interesting Scene On Board an East Indiaman, Showing the Effects of a Heavy Lurch, after Dinner, **after George Cruikshank, 1818**

The arduous voyage to Asia meant that the crew and passengers on East India ships spent long hours in close proximity. This caricature lampoons the variety of passengers, from army officers to women and children, that travelled on the Company's ships.

[PAG8632]

a 'prodigious sea' to ensure that things did not improve for Hickey, and as he later recorded: '[S]o ill was I that it was actually indifferent to me what became of the ship, and I should, I verily believe, have heard with composure that she was sinking.' Hickey was to recover his health and spirits by the time his ship reached Teneriffe, but like so many others he endured an extremely testing start to his passage to India.[17]

Besides ill health and stormy oceans, passengers had to come to terms with long days spent in the company of others from whom there was no escape. Life on board ship was often confined and claustrophobic, a situation

fig.74
On Board an Indiaman,
by Captain Robert Williams,
early 19th century
This scene shows a petty officer and crewman aboard the East Indiaman *Thames*. The artist commanded this ship on its voyage to Bombay and China in 1802. Typically, a commander earned £10 a month. By comparison, a boatswain, like the petty officer here, earned £3 10 shillings (£3.50), while a servant might make only 15 shillings (75p). Officers were permitted to supplement their income through private trade.

[BHC1080]

that created tensions, disputes and strained personal relations. Thomas Babington Macaulay neatly summarised how a voyage on an East Indiaman tested the patience and resolve of those on board:

Any thing is welcome which may break that long monotony, a sail, a shark, an albatross, a man overboard. Most passengers find some resource in eating twice as many meals as on land. But the great devices for killing time are quarrelling and flirting. The facilities for both these exciting pursuits are great. The inmates of the ship are thrown together far more than in any country-seat or boarding-house. None can escape but by imprisoning himself in a cell in which he can hardly turn. All food, all exercise is taken in company. Ceremony is to a great extent banished.[18]

One form of ceremony that was always observed on East Indiamen was that which took place when a ship crossed the Equator. When the *Plassey* 'crossed the line' in 1769, Hickey reported that 'all those who had never done so before paid the customary forfeit of a gallon of rum for the ship's crew, except Mr Smith the Scotch cadet, who not being overstocked with money to purchase the spirits, preferred submitting to the ceremony of ducking and shaving, which he went through to our infinite amusement'.[19] This ritual event was always a welcome break in the monotony of the voyage and, in an attempt to keep up the spirits of those on board, entertainments were sometimes organised in the form of concerts or plays. Maria, Lady Nugent reported that in 1811 the passengers on board the *Baring* put on a performance of *Macbeth*, and several songs were then sung by the ship's company: 'I enjoyed seeing the poor men enjoy their fête so much, for poor fellows! They have so much hard work and so little comfort on these long voyages!' Rather remarkably, later in the voyage the sailors acted out a translation of Molière's *Le Médecin malgré lui*, with Nugent commenting that '[t]he performance was very droll'.[20] Such occasions helped to while away some of the long days spent at sea, but it was always with very considerable relief that those on board East Indiamen caught first sight of their final destinations. Even then, arrivals in India were not always straightforward, especially for those who had to negotiate heavy surf before landing on the beach at Madras. This marked an often-uncomfortable transfer from ship to shore that served only to accentuate the extraordinary transition experienced as passengers moved between the maritime world and the imperial world of the East India Company, leaving behind the dark, damp confines of an East Indiaman for the bright light and relentlessly harsh climate of British India (figs 75 and 76).

fig. 75

Madras Landing, after J.B. East, 1837
The Company built warehouses, offices and even a church to serve the needs of its employees in Madras. As there was no natural harbour, passengers had to be taken ashore, from large European ships, in small surf boats.

[PAI0219]

fig. 76

Madras Embarking, after J.B. East, 1837
When Company servants returned to Britain with their families, they often brought an Indian woman, or *ayah,* to nurse the children. The Indian woman in the prow of this surf boat is probably on her way to Europe.

[PAI0220]

CONCLUSION

On the face of it, after 1750 the East India Company became preoccupied with empire as its military and political influence was extended far across the Indian subcontinent. As such it took on the trappings of imperial power by building forts, garrisons, courts, administrative buildings and elaborately constructed 'white towns' in Bombay, Madras and Calcutta (fig. 77). Yet, throughout, supporting the imperial edifice that had been constructed by men such as Clive, Hastings and Wellesley was an elaborate maritime trading system that continued to function, year in, year out, under the direction of those managing the Company's affairs at East India House. This ensured that, until it ceased trading in 1833, the Company remained a commercial enterprise at heart, dedicated to the transfer of goods, wealth and people between Britain and Asia. In that narrow sense, little had really changed since James Lancaster first set sail for the East Indies 232 years earlier.

fig. 77
Calcutta, after Henry Salt, 1809
As the Company concentrated its business interests in Bengal, in the north-east of India, the city of Calcutta developed on the River Hughli. It became one of the largest and most important urban centres in the country.

[PAI0192]

4

In trade as in warfare
Conflict and conquest in the Indian Ocean, 1600–1815

JOHN MCALEER

Sailing near the island of Pemba, off the coast of East Africa, the fourth East India Company voyage ran into problems with the local inhabitants. In response, Captain Alexander Sharpeigh ordered the capture of a number of their boats. The situation got much worse when the Africans were brought aboard the English ships. Once there, they attacked the European crew with knives, provoking a lethal response from the Company sailors: '[U]pon this occasion we made with them short work, and brought most of them by sundry ways to their last home; giving thanks to God for this last delivery, wherein the old proverb was verified, that one mischief comes seldom alone.' The goods found in the Africans' boats, consisting principally of coarse calicoes of no great value, were transferred to the *Ascension*, and the fleet went on its way.[1] As this example illustrates, violence and conflict often accompanied commercial endeavours. Indeed, the success of the East India Company and the armed protection and aggressive expansion of the trade on which it was based went hand in hand. In the first century of its existence, of any 'twenty ships sent out [from England] … scarce one returned' unless the Company 'sent three ships to protect one'.[2] Of course, the Company was not always at the receiving end of such plunder. As the experience of those Africans who encountered the *Ascension* highlights, the Company and its men frequently meted out the same treatment to troublesome European competitors and local traders alike.

Wars and conflicts among European neighbours also made an impact on the ways in which Company officials and sailors engaged with Asian merchants and princes. The prestige of a traveller, and that of his sovereign, was often based on his country's success in war. News travelled surprisingly quickly and widely in the early modern world. The kudos derived from martial prowess was not to be underestimated in extracting commercial concessions from Asian rulers. By displaying its ability to win on the battlefield, a country or a trading power could greatly increase its diplomatic standing in the eyes of Asian princes. For example, James Lancaster and his fleet were greeted at Aceh

fig. 78
Boat gun, 1793
This gun would have been used on board merchant ships. It has the letters 'VEIC' – the mark of the United East India Company – emblazoned on it.

[AAA2468]

by two Dutch merchants, who informed them that the local king 'was desirous to entertain' them and 'that the Queen of England was very famous in those parts, by reason of the wars and great victories which she had gotten against the king of Spain'.[3]

Of course, it was not only far-away conflicts that influenced the development of trade and affected the balance of political power in Asia. There were more direct examples of how warfare among Europeans (and between Europeans and indigenous people) impacted on Asian trade and relations. Skirmishes might be isolated incidents or part of wider, global conflicts. In either case, the outcome could have significant implications for where and with whom trade was carried on, and how it was conducted. In this way, indigenous people and rulers had a great say in the development of Company power and prestige. Similarly, the development of European trading companies in Asia was often violently resisted by local rulers and their subjects. This played an important part in shaping European interaction with these regions, as well as how people back in Europe viewed Asia. Through co-operation, collaboration and resistance, indigenous people at all levels helped to determine the direction of East India Company power and rule in Asia.

There was a direct connection between warfare and conflict on the one hand, and expanding East India Company interests in Asia on the other. Conflict grew in proportion to the expansion of the Company's commercial interests in the region, from the 17th century and throughout Britain's great age of global commercial consolidation in the 18th century. The interdependence between trading power and violence reached a brutal climax in the 19th century, when a series of military crises sent shockwaves through Company structures in Asia and eventually brought about its collapse, dissolution and replacement by British imperial government from Westminster (fig.78).

While a link between trade and military power throughout the period might seem obvious, it is much more difficult to pinpoint the precise nature of that relationship. The East India Company had its own armies but also relied, to a greater or lesser extent, on the forces of the Crown to assist in its domination of India. There was a similarly indeterminate alliance between the Company and the Royal Navy. The Company had its own navy – the Bombay Marine – which was created in the 17th century to protect Company trade from pirates operating off the Malabar and Makran Coasts of India, and in the Persian Gulf and the Red Sea. Known as the 'Bombay Buccaneers' by the Royal Navy, Company and Crown forces worked together to protect and extend British commercial and political interests in the region (fig.79).

fig.79
Howitzer, 18th century
This cannon is marked with the shield of the Company's coat of arms.

[KTP0022]

East India ships were constantly subjected to unwanted attention from European competitors. Rival Ottoman, Dutch and Portuguese vessels were continuously on the lookout for English ships laden with treasure or valuable cargo. The Company always took on ships 'in trade as in warfare', and these vessels carried the king's commission so that they could engage in fighting if required.[4] Throughout its history then, the Company's ships had a dual role: to open up East India Company trade and to defend it.

Sometimes, the battle for control of Asian trade did not even take place in the Indian Ocean itself. In October 1594, before the foundation of the Company, James Lancaster was ordered to plunder Pernambuco in north-eastern Brazil. The town was easily taken and, in an indication of the way Asian trade and commodities had spread around the planet even at that early date, Lancaster and his men captured the contents of a Portuguese carrack that had been unloaded for trans-shipment. They left for England the same evening with 15 ships, all laden with Portuguese East Indian treasure.[5]

Back in Asia, the battle for commercial concessions and trading privileges was no less intense. Captain Sharpeigh cautioned that ships needed firepower in order to carry out their trading unassailed. This would deter the Portuguese who 'lie at the Bar [at Surat], with 40 or 50 frigates, [so] that no boat can go in or out without their license'.[6] Lawrence Femell, on the sixth Company voyage, was warned to take 'special vigilance ... with regard to the Portugals'.[7] A few years later, in November 1612, the *Red Dragon* and *Hosiander*, under Captain Thomas Best, defeated a Portuguese fleet of four galleons and 26 frigates under Admiral Nuño de Cunha. Ralph Crosse, purser of the *Hosiander*, gave an account of Best's action at Surat. His fleet was anchored off the bar when, on 27 November 1612, news arrived that a Portuguese expedition had sailed from Goa with orders to capture the English. Captain Best prepared the vessels for action, making sure that 'every man was ready with great spirit and courage to encounter the enemy'. The Portuguese vastly outnumbered the English; Crosse estimated that they had some 2,000 men at their disposal, while the English numbered 'little more than 200 in both our ships; but the Lord I hope will fight for us, in whom is our trust in the day of battle'. Despite their numerical disadvantage, Captain Best roused his men saying that 'although their forces were more than ours, yet they were both base and cowardly.... He did persuade every man to be of good courage and show ourselves true Englishmen, famous over all the world for true valour; and that God in whom we trusted would be our help.'[8] In 1622, the East India Company defeated the Portuguese again, when five of their ships supported a Persian raid on the Portuguese base off Hormuz. This gave them privileged access to Persian ports. Conflict with the Portuguese effectively ceased in 1635, and Bombay was presented to Charles II as part of Catherine of Braganza's dowry in 1661, with the Company being granted the site in 1668.

The most potent threat to English activity in Asia in the 17th century, however, came from the Dutch. Edward Barlow thought they were 'stronger in the East Indies than all the other Christian nations', having '150 or 200 sail of ships and 30,000 men or servants always in pay'.[9] Indeed, the dominance of the Dutch East India Company effectively relegated the English to bit-part players in the Asian trade throughout the century. In 1604, a Company voyage commanded by Sir Henry Middleton reached the islands of Ternate, Tidore, Ambon and Banda (in present-day Indonesia). In Banda, they encountered severe hostility from the Dutch East India Company, the VOC, which heralded the beginning of Anglo-Dutch competition for access to spices. The English were particularly wary of the Dutch reputation for sharp business practices. Thomas Roe expressed the fears of many early Company officials and directors when he worried that they 'would out-present, out-bribe and out-buy us in all things'.[10] Conflict with the Dutch was the inevitable result of the VOC's attempts to enforce the exclusive trading rights they had extracted from various rulers in the Spice Islands. From 1609, the Dutch prevented English ships from trading freely in the Molucca Islands. In response, from 1611 to 1617, the English retaliated, attempting to establish trading posts elsewhere in the region, which blatantly threatened the Dutch dominance of East Indies trade. Diplomatic agreements in Europe in 1620 supposedly ushered in a period of co-operation between the two countries but it did little to change the reality on the ground.

The ratcheting up of tension over a period of twenty years ended with the infamous 'Amboina massacre'. On trumped-up charges of organising a coup, ten English merchants at the Amboina factory, in the Spice Islands, were executed by the Dutch in 1623. Although this caused outrage in Europe and precipitated a diplomatic crisis, the English quietly withdrew from most of their trading activities in this region and focused on other Asian interests. In strategic terms, it forced the English to concentrate on India, a previously underexploited source of textiles and spices. Even the withdrawal of the English from the Dutch-controlled Spice Islands did little to quell the simmering rivalry between the two powers. Throughout the 17th century, the English and Dutch East India Companies fought for control of trade in Asia as part of a larger tussle for the leadership of Protestant Europe. The continued enmity between the countries boiled over into full-scale war three times during the course of the 17th century. Sometimes the conflict during these 'Anglo-Dutch' wars was very close to home and the seat of governmental power, such as the audacious Dutch raid up the River Medway, close to London, in June 1667. But fighting also took place on

the other side of the world. During the Third Anglo-Dutch War (1672–74), for example, an East India Company fleet of ten ships was sailing from Masulipatam to Madras under Captain William Basse in the *London* in late August 1673. When they encountered a Dutch fleet of 14 men-of-war, the fighting lasted nearly six hours. It resulted in the complete defeat of the English, with the loss of three ships and the capture of about 300 men.[11]

Edward Barlow's career illustrates the ways in which these wars affected the lives of individual sailors. He had served as a seaman in the Royal Navy in European waters during the Second Anglo-Dutch War (1664–67), seeing action at the Battle of Lowestoft in 1665 and the Four Days' Fight in June 1666. By the time of the Third Anglo-Dutch War, Barlow was in the service of the East India Company. Sailing from Gravesend on 27 September 1671, he visited Bantam and Taiwan. In the autumn of 1672, however, he was captured by the Dutch in the Bangka Strait. He and his companions knew nothing of the outbreak of war, and found themselves outnumbered eight to one. Following a brief skirmish, the English flag was struck and the Dutchmen came on board, 'all armed, and told us how they had both wars with the English and French, and that we were their prize'. The prospect of falling prey to the Dutch was not an appealing one 'seeing that in an instant all our goods, chests, and clothes, and ship and all, were made prize of, and we ourselves prisoners, and for how long we could not tell'. Barlow mused that men, whose goods 'were worth £500 or £600 or £1000 not half an hour before, were then not worth a penny, all [goods] being made prize of and nothing left us but the old clothes upon our backs'. It was during his time as a prisoner of war in Batavia that Barlow taught himself to write and began the journal, which constitutes his claim to fame (fig.80). The taunting by their Dutch captors, as reported by Barlow, illustrates how European religious controversies and political intrigues of the time found expression as far away as Asia: 'They called us all rogues and dogs that could be, and gave many uncivil and scandalous speeches against our King for taking the French's part, saying that he would turn papist and that he would have his head cut off as his father's was – calling all the bad names against him they could invent for breaking peace.'[12]

Of course, at the same time as Europeans were fighting over trade, politics and religion, so their representatives in Asia were also involved in conflicts of their own in attempts to elicit greater profits for their employers or security for themselves. In March 1686, Robert Knox was commissioned to take part in the East India Company's war against the Mughal emperor Aurangzeb in Bengal. During his time in Ceylon, he had witnessed the Kingdom of Kandy waging wars against various Europeans who were trying to encroach on Kandian territory. The Kandians frequently got the upper hand on their foreign aggressors:

fig.80
The Manner of Our Unfortunate Being Taken by the Dutch in the Straights of Banka in the Latitude 2 & 3 Degrees, **by Edward Barlow, 17th century** Edward Barlow and his shipmates were captured in South-East Asia by the Dutch in 1672, as part of the ongoing Third Anglo-Dutch War. [JOD/4/78]

By the long wars first between them and the Portuguese, and since with the Hollander, they have had such ample experience, as hath much improved them in the art of War above what they were formerly. And many of the chief commanders and leaders of their armies are men which formerly served the Portuguese against them. By which they come to know the disposition and discipline of Christian armies. Insomuch as they have given the Dutch several overthrows, and taken Forts from them, which they had up in the Country.[13]

PIRACY

It was not just violence from organised sources that could threaten East India Company trade: piracy was a significant problem for fleets throughout the period. The entire course of the trade route from Europe to Asia and back again was fraught with danger from bandits on the high seas, and led the Company's directors to give specific and detailed orders to captains as to which routes they should take. For example, the Company ordered its ships to steer at least 30 leagues west of Madeira to avoid Barbary pirates preying there. But indigenous groups in Asia, such as the Angrians based on the Malabar Coast of India, also made Company captains and shareholders nervous. The main hunting grounds for such groups were the west coast of India, the Mozambique Channel, the mouth of the Red Sea and the Persian Gulf, all of which they patrolled in search of treasure-laden victims. As a result, Company vessels were always armed and expected to defend themselves: Lancaster's ships mounted 40 guns on the first Company voyage.

The Company faced such threats from these marauders that a 'Marine' force was established, initially to defend trading and pilgrim vessels. On 20 March 1698, three armed vessels convoyed a Mughal fleet back to Surat in safety. As an indication of the precarious nature of merchant shipping at the time, during this voyage the notorious pirate Captain William Kidd passed close to them. Kidd was originally sent out in the *Adventure Galley* (30 guns), via New York, to catch pirates but he turned rover himself. He continued to Rajahpore, off which port he plundered a vessel registered at Bombay. After careening at the Laccadive Islands, he proceeded to Calicut, in India. Here, Kidd took another vessel and made his escape by pretending to be a Company ship. At Cochin, he captured three valuable Dutch prizes then retired to St Mary's, an island off the east coast of Madagascar, where the pirates had established fortified stations and where they received stores from New York and the West Indies.[14]

Among those sailors who found themselves having a close encounter with William Kidd was Edward Barlow, although he only found out the identity of his assailant afterwards. It led him to remark on the way that pirates operated in the Indian Ocean:

[The pirates] generally fit ships and sloops in the West Indies and at New York and at the Bermudas, and pretend they are going for Guinea, but come for the island of St Lawrence, and there meet one another and join and make their rendezvous there and, as it is said, carry all their booty there till such time as they have sufficient; and then many of them return home and skulk about and keep out of the way, but some of them now and then are taken and hanged for their pains.[15]

As captain of the *Septer*, Barlow was at Mocha to protect pilgrim ships returning to Surat from attack by European pirates. Shortly after setting out on the voyage, he sighted a strange ship in the convoy. Her unusual rigging caught his attention — she seemed to be a galley with a tier of ports for oars on her lower deck. As there was little wind, Barlow ordered the *Septer* towards the ship, which had already begun firing on one of the larger ships in the convoy. As the *Septer* came up firing, the mysterious vessel hauled off. After waiting for a while out of range, she made all sail and went off. It was only later that Barlow discovered that it was William Kidd's *Adventure Galley*.

The problem of piracy persisted into the 18th century. In August 1713, a Mr Travers applied to the directors of the East India Company to send a trading expedition to Mozambique and Madagascar. For this privilege, he was willing to pay the Company three per cent on the gross sale of the returned cargo. In making his representation to the committee and seeking their support, Travers acknowledged that his ship would need to be 'extraordinary strong to proceed on said voyage', which is why he proposed building a 200-ton frigate of 16 guns for the purpose. In the end, however, the Company declined to support the venture, fearing that the ship might be 'sold to or surprised by the Pyrates', which operated around the southern waters of Africa, and thereby endangering the Company's ships carrying the fruits of its Asian trade back to Britain.[16] This was not an idle concern. In June 1720, William Gordon and John Huggins brought a similar proposal 'for opening and carrying on a great and profitable Trade on the South East Coast of Africa and Islands adjacent hitherto not entered into'.[17] In rejecting this proposal, the problem of unlicensed and piratical activity again entered into the consideration of the Company's directors. On 22 June, five days after hearing Gordon and Huggins's case, the Court of Directors noted a letter by James Naish 'super cargo of the Ostend ship *House of Austria*', which had apparently been plundered off the Cape the previous February by a ship called the *Dragon*. This ship was, according to the Company's sources, 'commanded by an English Pyrate by the name of Captain Congdon' and it 'carried forty guns, twenty brass pieces upon swivels, 320 men and small arms for twice that number'.[18]

The danger posed by European pirates and the assaults carried out by individual Asian adventurers were matters of significant concern to the

Commodore Sir William James, **by Sir Joshua Reynolds, 1784**
This painting was made for James's widow after the death of her husband. As well as commissioning this portrait, she also built Severndroog Castle, near Greenwich, in his memory.

[BHC2801]

East India Company. However, a much greater risk to Company power and profits was posed by the outbreak of full-scale war between European countries.

WAR AND CONFLICT IN THE 18TH CENTURY

Britain and France were at war on numerous occasions during the 18th century. This was also the period in which British East India Company trade grew at an exponential rate, with demand for textiles and tea sustaining huge profits for the Company. Although large and technically equipped to defend themselves, the Company's vessels were rather inadequate for the task. Theoretically, they could carry guns for defence against pirates, privateers and small warships. Indeed, from a distance, they appeared quite similar to a small ship of the line, a deception usually reinforced by paintwork and dummy cannon. They were not, however, capable of fighting off an enemy frigate or ship of the line under normal circumstances, because their guns were usually of inferior design, and their crew smaller and less well trained than those on a naval ship. East India ships sought to ensure the safety of their cargo and passengers, not to defeat enemy warships in battle.

To defend itself from piracy and other enemies in the seas around India, the Company relied on its maritime 'police force', which came to be called the Bombay Marine. The Company had first formed a 'Marine' as early as 1613. A local force of small boats, mounting between two and six guns each, was established to defend Company trade from Surat, and for convoying purposes. By 1669, trade at Bombay had been so much exposed to the attacks of Malabar pirates that three small, armed vessels were constructed. By 1716, its duties of convoying ships in trade cost £51,700 per annum and it consisted of one ship of 32 guns, four medium-sized 'grab-ships' (20 to 28 guns) and 20 small 'grab' and 'galivats' (5 to 12 guns).[19]

The Bombay Marine was mainly responsible for clearing the coasts of so-called pirates. One such example of this is the action taken by Commodore Sir William James. James's capture of Severndroog Fort in 1755 is commemorated in Sir Joshua Reynolds's three-quarter-length portrait of 1784 (fig.81), a copy commissioned by James's widow of an earlier painting. After serving in India, James became a notable figure in East India Company operations in London, serving as chairman of the Company for some 20 years. However, here he is shown in the full-dress uniform of a commodore of the Bombay Marine. He had joined the service of the East India Company in 1747 and became commodore of its marine forces four years later. James is shown here holding a plan of the stronghold of

fig.82
A View of Geriah,
after M. Hore, c.1756
This shows the taking of Geriah, the
Maratha pirates' capital on the west
coast of India, by a British fleet
under the command of Admirals
Watson and Pocock on 13 February
1756.

[PAF4591]

Severndroog in his hand. James's actions were part of a wider global conflict:
the Seven Years' War.

In the middle years of the 18th century, the Bombay Presidency decided
to make a determined attempt to rid the west coast of India of the pirate
threat. James had already beaten off a powerful Angrian attack on a fleet of
70 traders, which he was escorting from Bombay to the north of Goa. The
help of the Marathas, the regional power in this part of India, was sought for
a combined military and naval attack on the Angrian stronghold of
Severndroog. The Angrians were led by descendants of Kanhoji Angre, a
naval commander under the Marathas who had subsequently gone renegade.
A treaty was concluded by which the British agreed to blockade Severndroog
harbour to prevent the Angrian fleet bringing aid to the fort, while the
Marathas stormed the fort from the landward side. Commodore James, in
his flagship the 44-gun *Protector*, led the squadron. They were joined by a
Maratha fleet carrying 10,000 soldiers. While the Maratha army showed little

taste for battle, James was determined that the assault should not end in stalemate. He sent boats to reconnoitre and, after positive reports about the depth of the water, James manoeuvred the *Protector* into a position between the fort and the mainland. Under heavy fire, he directed her broadsides at Severndroog, while musketeers in the tops dispersed the gunners in the main fort. After a four-hour bombardment, a magazine in the fort blew up, and most of the fleeing garrison were taken prisoner by the British ships.

The Seven Years' War, of which James's action was a part, was the first worldwide battle for empire with two superpowers – Britain and France – contesting global dominance. Although battles in the Atlantic and Mediterranean theatres, as well as on the fields of Germany, had the most direct impact on the outcome of the war, events in Asia were equally momentous for the future direction of the East India Company. Successes, such as the capture of Geriah in February 1756 (fig. 82), were crucial in providing a springboard for the Company's eventual control of most of the Indian subcontinent. For the East India Company, British victory over the French in the Seven Years' War went together with newly acquired dominance in its principal commercial base: Bengal. At the same time as Britain was flexing its imperial muscles in the 1750s, the Mughal Empire in India was in an advanced state of decay. Regional states emerged across India and the Company began to get involved in local power politics, partly to renegotiate its various commercial treaties. It raised its own armies and prepared for war. The Company's base at Calcutta was taken by one of those regional power brokers, the Nawab of Bengal, in 1756. But a year later a force under Robert Clive recaptured the city and, following victory at the Battle of Plassey, the Company replaced the nawab with its own preferred candidate. Having seen off the rival French during the course of the Seven Years' War, the Company assumed the *diwani* of Bengal in 1765. The East India Company was now a regional power in India, responsible for the civil, judicial and revenue administration of India's richest province, with some 20 million inhabitants.

Even with the assistance of the Bombay Marine, the East India Company relied heavily on the protection of the Royal Navy throughout this period. A combination of Royal Navy ships, their Bombay Marine counterparts, and heavily armed East Indiamen presented a significant arsenal ranged against would-be predators. The actions of Captain John Allen of the East India ship *Duke of Dorset*, commemorated in a silver cup and cover presented to him (fig. 83), highlight the multiple roles that a Company commander was

fig. 83
Presentation cup,
by William Cripps, 1761–62
This silver cup was presented by the East India Company to John Allen, of the Company's ship *Duke of Dorset*, for his part in repulsing a Dutch raid on the River Ganges.
[PLT0003]

expected to play. One side of the cup bears a cartouche with the engraved coat of arms of the East India Company and the motto 'Auspicio Regis et Senatus Angliæ' ('By the Command of the King and Parliament of England'). The inscription on the other side gives more details of the circumstances of its presentation, referring to Allen's 'Gallant Behaviour against the Dutch in Bengal River in the Year 1759'. On 24 November 1759, Captain Wilson of the *Calcutta* led several British East Indiamen in a successful attack on seven Dutch ships which had attempted to seize Chinsura, on the River Ganges. When Bernard Forrester, captain of the *Duke of Dorset*, was disabled in the knee by grapeshot early in the engagement, First Mate John Allen took command. After Forrester's death the following March, Allen's promotion to command of the *Duke of Dorset* was confirmed. The East India Company was particularly generous in rewarding its officers and men, and the crews of the *Calcutta*, *Hardwick* and *Duke of Dorset* received the sum of £2,000 per ship for their part in the action. The East India Company Court minutes for 19 February 1762 record the decision 'that Capt. John Allen have likewise a gratuity to the value of Fifty Guineas (in addition to what he has received as Chief Mate) for his brave Conduct in the *Duke of Dorset* in the above engagement on Capt. Forrester the former Commander of that ship being disabled'.[20] The Company had always looked after and rewarded its servants well for protecting its property and interests. Clement Downing, who served in the Bombay Marine, felt that the East India Company was 'worthy to be served above all the merchants in Great Britain for the care they take of those who receive damage, and also for the widows of those who are killed in the service'.[21]

CONSOLIDATING POWER: THE LATE 18TH CENTURY

Shortly after the conclusion of the Seven Years' War, British power in the Indian Ocean was under threat again. This time the source of strife came from 'within' the empire, with the outbreak of rebellion in 13 colonies of the Americas. Seizing this opportunity, the French and Dutch set about pressurising British shipping in every corner of the globe. The Battle of Negapatam of 1782, depicted here by Dominic Serres the Elder (fig. 84), is just one example of this. In this image, Serres painted the type of naval engagement that was commonplace in the 18th century. It was the third of five fleet battles fought off the Coromandel Coast of south-east India, near Ceylon, during the War of American Independence. It pitted the French Admiral Suffren against Sir Edward Hughes's East Indies squadron of the Royal Navy. With a fleet comprising 12 ships of the line and four frigates,

Suffren caught up with Hughes in the harbour of Negapatam on 5 July. Hughes made use of the onset of a squall to sail out of the harbour, however, so that the two fleets spent the night anchored just two cannon shots apart. The next morning, 6 July, the fleets closed and opened fire on each other. The battle proceeded with vigour until about one o'clock, when the wind changed suddenly, throwing both sides into confusion. Hughes attempted to reform his line, but neither fleet was in a state to adopt battle positions easily, so Suffren decided to draw away towards Cuddalore. Both admirals were tenacious fighters: 77 men were killed on the British side with 233 wounded, while French fatalities numbered 178 with 600 wounded. A well-born Frenchman from Gascony, the artist's own life tells us much about the upheavals convulsing Europe in the late 18th century. Serres ran away to sea rather than follow his family's wish that he enter the Church. He probably arrived in England as a naval prisoner of war, took up painting and settled there. He painted many scenes of maritime battle, often for people involved in the action itself. This painting, for example, belonged to Hughes.

The last great global conflict of the 18th century – the struggles between Britain and Revolutionary and Napoleonic France – also had significant ramifications for the position of the East India Company in Asia. Napoleon instructed his officials to 'maintain a cordial connection with the people and princes groaning under the yoke of the East India Company', and to be watchful for an opportunity to strike against 'the tyrants of India'.[22] The Battle of Pulo Aor was one of the most important in that war, in the Asian arena at least. It encapsulates many of the reasons why the East India Company and its trade were so intimately bound up with the national interest, as well as how it managed to protect its commercial power. The battle itself took place off the islet of Pulau Aur (otherwise 'Pulo Aor'), in the Straits of Malacca, and illustrates French strategy in the Indian Ocean. Captain Nathaniel Dance (fig. 85) was the main protagonist in the action. He had entered the East India Company's service in 1759 and made nine voyages to India between 1759 and 1781. Moving steadily up through the Company's ranks, he was eventually appointed commander of the *Lord Camden* in 1786, making his last voyage to Asia as commander of another ship with a similar name, the *Earl Camden*, in 1802. In 1804 Dance was, by virtue of his seniority, commodore of the Company's homeward-bound fleet, which sailed from Canton on 31 January and consisted of 16 regular, 1,200-ton East India ships, 11 country ships and the *Ganges*, a fast-sailing brig.

In the Straits of Malacca, off Pulo Aor, on 14 February, this fleet engaged a French squadron of four warships under Admiral Linois. Linois, in the *Marengo*, had been ordered there by Napoleon in order to attack British shipping on the resumption of hostilities between the two countries. The French commander had served in the East Indies under Suffren. In 1803 he

fig. 84 *(overleaf)*
Battle of Negapatam, 6 July 1782,
by Dominic Serres the Elder, 1786
This battle was one of a number that took place between British and French fleets off the coast of India as they fought for control of European trade in the region.

[BHC0448]

CONFLICT AND CONQUEST IN THE INDIAN OCEAN, 1600–1815

returned to the Indian Ocean, before the official declaration of war, under orders to install garrisons in the French and Dutch colonies in the region and to prey on lightly defended British merchant shipping. The British fleet leaving China in early 1804 was carrying tea worth some £3 million, while the fleet was valued at more than £7 million.[23] But Dance's ingenious tactics (fig. 86) succeeded in driving off the powerful French naval squadron. Although no warships protected the convoy, Dance knew that lookouts could, from a distance, mistake a large East Indiaman for a ship of the line. He raised flags indicating that his fleet included part of the Royal Navy squadron operating in the Indian Ocean at the time, and he formed his notional squadron into a line of battle. Although Linois's ships were clearly superior, the British reaction unnerved him and he quickly broke off combat. He believed that he was engaged with ships of the line and did not notice that they were lightly armed merchant ships. The next morning, thinking he was in the presence of a superior force, he fired a few broadsides and fled. On the British side, one man was killed and another wounded, both on board the *Royal George*; the other ships sustained no damage. Dance continued his ruse, pursuing Linois for two hours until the convoy was safe. Linois's fleet got its comeuppance, the Society of East India Commanders gleefully observed, for provoking 'a contest with the old English valour, by which it was defeated'.[24]

The *Naval Chronicle* expressed the general view of the fleet's action: 'By its unprecedented success it has added to our national fame; and by its preservation of so vast a property, at this juncture, it has added to our means of security and strengthened our sinews of war.'[25] For his part in the action, Dance was lauded as a national hero. George III knighted him for his courage, and various mercantile and patriotic organisations awarded him large sums of money. He was presented with £5,000 by the Bombay Insurance Company and a pension of £500 a year by the East India Company. He was also made a present of 2,000 guineas and plate worth 200 guineas by the Company. On 14 August 1804, Lloyd's Patriotic Fund resolved unanimously:

That the circumstance of an enemy's fleet of ships of war, commanded by an Admiral in an 84 gun ship, being defeated and chased by a fleet of Merchantmen, protecting an immense property, is highly honourable to the British naval character, and affords a brilliant example to the present and future ages.[26]

They voted Dance a sword and a silver vase, valued at £100 each. At a special meeting, called on 22 August at the Jerusalem Coffee House, the Society of East India Commanders commissioned a portrait of Nathaniel Dance and a painting of the action at Pulo Aor, saying they 'had judged this Action to surpass credibility, when the intelligence of it first reached England'.[27] Meanwhile, both Linois's own officers and the Emperor

fig. 85
Sir Nathaniel Dance,
by John Raphael Smith,
1 January 1805
Nathaniel Dance was the commander of a homeward-bound fleet of East Indiamen, laden with valuable cargo from China, which encountered and defeated a fleet of French warships.

[PAH5517]

THE CHINA FLEET
heavily laden,
Commanded by
COMMODORE SIR NATHANIEL DANCE,
beating off
Adm.ᵗ Linois and his Squadron
the 15ᵗʰ of Feb.ʸ 1804.

fig. 86

The China Fleet ... Commanded by Commodore Sir Nathaniel Dance, after Thomas Butterworth, 25 November 1804

This action, off Pulo Aor in the Straits of Malacca, saved a fleet of East Indiamen worth over £7 million from capture by a French squadron under Admiral Linois.

[PAG9019]

J. Clark & H. Merke sculp.

List of Ships

English	French Force
1. Royal George	a. Marengo Flag Ship of 84 Guns.
2. Ganges.	b. La Belle Poule Frigate of 50 Guns.
3. Camden.	c. La Semillante Frigate of 44 Guns.
4. Alfred.	d. A Corvette of 28 Guns.
5. Coutts	e. A Dutch Brig of 18 Guns.
6. E. Abergaveny.	
7. Cumberland.	
8. Addington.	
9. Wexford.	
10. Warley.	
11. Hope.	
12. Dorsetshire.	
13. Exeter.	
14. Ocean.	
15. Warren Hastings.	
16. Bombay Castle.	

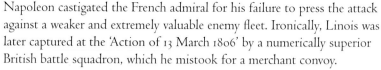

fig. 87

Lloyd's Patriotic Fund vase, by Digby Scott and Benjamin Smith, 1806

This silver vase was given to John Timins, an East India Company captain, for his role in defeating the French at the Battle of Pulo Aor. The Patriotic Fund was founded at a meeting at Lloyd's Coffee House in 1803. It gave awards of merit in the form of money, silver and presentation swords. The sculptor John Flaxman produced the final design for the vases.

[PLT0180]

Napoleon castigated the French admiral for his failure to press the attack against a weaker and extremely valuable enemy fleet. Ironically, Linois was later captured at the 'Action of 13 March 1806' by a numerically superior British battle squadron, which he mistook for a merchant convoy.

Dance was not the only person who played a role in the action, or who was recognised afterwards. Captain John Fam Timins, who had previously served in the Royal Navy, was heartily commended for 'the gallant manner in which he led the action and placed the *Royal George* alongside the French Admiral's Ship, the *Marengo*'.[28] In addition to the £50 presented to the commanders of the other ships in the action, Timins received a silver vase with an appropriate inscription (fig. 87). On one side, the lower section is inscribed with the words 'Britannia Triumphant' and shows a figure of Britannia holding winged Victory in her hand. The other side depicts Hercules slaying the Hydra, with the legend 'Britons Strike Home' (the motto of the Lloyd's Patriotic Fund). Lieutenant Robert Fowler of the Royal Navy, who was a passenger on board the *Earl Camden*, 'afforded Captain Dance very material assistance' during the engagement. In recognition of this, the Court of Directors of the East India Company decided to present Fowler with 'the sum of three hundred guineas, for the purchase of a piece of plate as an acknowledgement of the sense they entertain of his service on the occasion'.[29] He was also awarded a sword, to the value of £50, by the Lloyd's Patriotic Fund (figs 88 and 89).

France continued to wage war on Britain. Indeed, Napoleon's designs on India, demonstrated by his expedition to Egypt, clearly illustrate how valuable and important Asian trade was to Britain. As with the China fleet, the trading world of the East India Company had become symbiotically connected to Britain's broader political concerns. One response from the British government to French threats to India was to secure the Indian Ocean ever more tightly, drawing more and more of it within its sphere of influence. The Cape of Good Hope, for example, was captured as a means of preventing 'what had been a mere feather in the hands of Holland [becoming] a sword in the hands of France'.[30] Elsewhere the same calculations were taking place. The fall of Mauritius in 1810 was regarded by Lord Minto, the governor general of India, as one of the most important services 'that could be rendered to the East India Company and the nation in the east'.[31]

The capture of the Cape and Mauritius should have neutralised any remaining French threat. But events in Europe overtook developments in the East. In 1810, France formally annexed the Netherlands. Dutch possessions

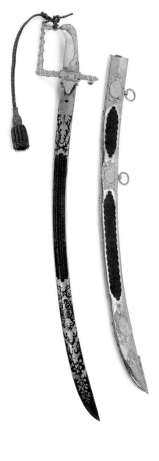

figs 88 and 89
**Presentation swords,
by Richard Teed, 1804**
These swords were awarded by
Lloyd's Patriotic Fund to Lieutenant
Robert Fowler of the Royal Navy
and Captain Henry Wilson of the
East Indiaman *Warley*, respectively.
Their actions were instrumental in
defeating the French at Pulo Aor.

[ZBA1470 and WPN1042]

CONFLICT AND CONQUEST IN THE INDIAN OCEAN, 1600–1815

in the East Indies were now potential bases from which France could launch an assault on British and Company interests in India. Royal Navy ships were duly deployed to combat the threat. Captain Sir Christopher Cole (fig.90) made his reputation in 1810 when he captured Neira, the principal Dutch possession in the Banda Islands. He had been in the East Indies since 1804, when he arrived as flag captain to Sir Edward Pellew in the *Culloden*. In this portrait, he is depicted wearing the gold medal awarded to him for his services in taking Neira.

Cole also took a leading part in the capture of Java in 1811, when an amphibious British force seized the Dutch island to prevent its use as a French naval base. A British force, comprising some 81 ships, sailed from India in April 1811. The escorting fleet consisted of four ships of the line, 14 frigates and seven sloops of war and corvettes. Some 12,000 troops were embarked, half of them Indian troops serving in armies of the East India Company. This image (fig.91) shows a boat action off the coast of Java led by Captain Robert Maunsell, and illustrates how amphibious actions operated at the time. On 31 July 1811, Maunsell, in command of the sloop *Procris*, discovered a convoy of 40 or 50 *proas* (Javanese canoes) escorted by six French gunboats in the mouth of the Indromayo River. When he closed to within a gunshot in shallow water, he found that his fire made little impression on the gunboats. So he launched his boats and two flatboats, with 40 men. They were able to board and capture five of the French gunboats in quick succession, while the sixth blew up. Meanwhile, the convoy escaped up the shallow muddy river. Despite this inconclusive action, however, the island eventually surrendered and the threat to Company business in the eastern seas was averted. Admiral Sir Nesbit Josiah Willoughby wrote to the Admiralty in October 1811 setting out the position:

I am extremely happy to congratulate their lordships upon the conquest of the valuable island of Java and its dependencies, wherein the evils adverted to are done away by the total fall of all the enemy's settlements in the East, and on taking possession of Macassar and Coupang on the Island of Timor, the French flag will no longer fly in the Eastern Seas.[32]

With the capture of Java, the naval war in the East was at an end.

However, British rule in India was not only subject to assault by European rivals. Local Asian rulers were constantly trying to check the Company's advance, as it sought to expand inland from its fortified strongholds on the coast. One of the most successful challenges to Company power was that posed by the sultans of Mysore. Initially led by Hyder Ali, the Mysoreans fought four wars with the British, over successive generations, for control of southern India. They were formidable foes. In September 1780, at the beginning of the Second Anglo-Mysore War, Tipu Sultan,

fig.90
Captain Sir Christopher Cole,
by Margaret Carpenter, 1820–24
Captain Cole is depicted wearing the gold medal that he received for leading the British assault against the Dutch in the Banda Islands in 1810. He played a leading part in capturing Java the following year.

[BHC2623]

CONFLICT AND CONQUEST IN THE INDIAN OCEAN, 1600–1815

fig. 91
*Captain Robert Maunsell Capturing
French Gunboats off Java, July 1811,*
by **William John Huggins**, *c.*1812
The battle between Britain and
France for global dominance at the
beginning of the 19th century
extended as far as Java. In capturing
the island, the British prevented the
French from using it as a base to
attack India.

[BHC4218]

fig. 92

Plan of the attack by Lord Cornwallis on Seringapatam, 1792
East India Company troops, together with Crown forces, fought a number of wars against the rulers of Mysore in southern India. Seringapatam, the capital of Mysore, was besieged in 1792.

[GREN 71/7]

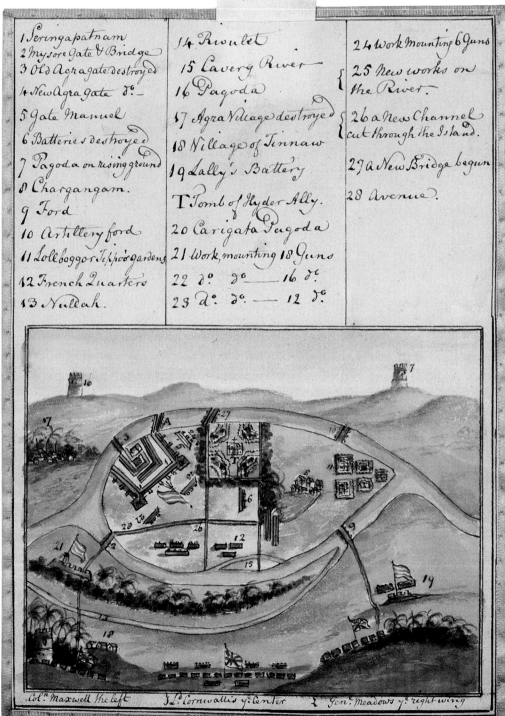

Hyder's son and successor, defeated Colonel Baillie at the Battle of Pollilur, killing some 3,000 British troops in the process. Sir Hector Munro described it as 'the severest blow that the English ever sustained in India'.[33] Even when they managed to lay siege to the Mysore capital, Seringapatam, in 1792, the British could not defeat Tipu (fig.92). As befitted his self-image as an important potentate, Tipu was alive to the niceties of the etiquette of war and tried to impress his enemies with his munificence. While Lord Cornwallis besieged his capital, Tipu sent out a procession of 200 men carrying large dishes of kebabs, curries and spiced meats. Unfortunately, Cornwallis had 'no relish for Eastern cookery', though his men had no such complaints.[34]

It took a large concerted action, by a combined army consisting of Crown and Company troops, eventually to defeat Tipu in 1799, when Seringapatam finally fell. The city was stormed in May 1799 by troops under Sir David Baird, who had also fought Tipu's father. Tipu was killed defending his capital city. His body was discovered, shot through the head, under a pile of other bodies. Property to the value of over £1 million was seized. The defeat of Tipu removed one of the last obstacles to the spread of British rule across the subcontinent. His heroic death, as well as the wealth of his court, made him a well-known figure in Britain – often held up as the exemplar of the typical Oriental 'despot'. He quickly assumed celebrity status and was portrayed in all sorts of ways. HMS *Seringapatam*, a 46-gun fifth-rate (frigate) built for the Royal Navy at Bombay Dockyard in 1819, incorporated a reference to the vanquished ruler (fig.93). Part of the ship's carving included a seated figure wearing a turban, which probably represents Tipu. He is riding a *roc*, a mythical bird of great strength. This, together with the umbrella he holds, is a symbol of his regal status. Tipu also left a legacy among the people of India, many of whom tried to resist the rule of the East India Company and sought to use him as inspiration.

CONCLUSION: THE ESTABLISHMENT OF THE INDIAN NAVY IN 1830

By 1830, the East India Company was in control of large swathes of India. In that year, the Company's naval force was renamed 'His Majesty's Indian Navy'. Captain Sir Robert Oliver, a former naval officer, became superintendent of the Indian Navy in 1837. He held the post until his death

fig.93
**Figurehead from
HMS *Seringapatam*, 1819**
This carving probably represents Tipu Sultan, the ruler of Mysore. He was eventually defeated by a combination of Company and Crown forces in 1799.
[FHD0102]

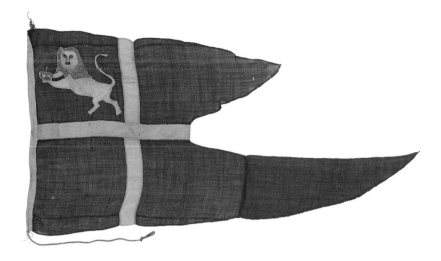

in 1848. The new naval force had the same trappings as national navies, such as flags and uniforms (figs 94 and 95). As the 19th century ushered in an era of global dominance for Britain, the Indian Navy spent less of its time defending trade from pirates and other European rivals. By the time the East India Company lost the last of its trading monopolies – to China in 1833 – the Indian Navy was widely employed in conducting scientific expeditions, charting coastlines and surveying seabeds.

Yet, war and conflict did not disappear, or become less of a concern to the East India Company. While they were shorn of any commercial tasks, the directors of the East India Company and their servants in India were now responsible for administering an entire subcontinent. British power in India had developed, from the late 18th century onwards, through an uneasy alliance between the Company and the British government in London. Despite the apparently diminished threat to British commercial and political power, therefore, India and the adjacent Indian Ocean region was still vital to British strategic interests. A series of crises, culminating in the Indian Mutiny of 1857, would strike at the very heart of East India Company rule in India. Ultimately, the initial success of the Company in defending, developing and expanding its trade would lead to its demise and replacement by private trading concerns in the commercial arena and the British government in political affairs.

5

Smoke, and flame, and thunder

The Company, its demise and its legacies,
*c.*1830–70

ROBERT J. BLYTH

When the East India Company lost its trading monopoly with China in 1833, it ceased to be a major commercial enterprise. The Charter Act of that year required the Company to 'close their commercial business, and make sale of all their merchandize and effects at home and abroad' by 22 April 1834.[1] Shorn of its trading arm, the Company was now principally responsible for the government of a vast and growing Indian empire that sprawled across much of the subcontinent and beyond. Its continued involvement with India, as a semi-independent branch of government, was increasingly seen by many in Britain as anachronistic and incompatible with emerging Victorian ideas about the form and purpose of the British Empire. In what was to prove the final quarter century of the Company's long existence, it was shaken not only by mounting hostility at home, but also by a series of dramatic, bloody and shattering events in Asia.

THE FIRST CHINA WAR

As a consequence of its long monopoly over trade with China, the Company acted as a British 'gatekeeper' at Canton. It policed Britain's relationship with Chinese officials, merchants and the imperial court. Indeed, the importance of the Company's role in mediating Anglo-Chinese affairs was recognised in the British government's willingness to maintain the China monopoly until 1833. By that date, however, the pressure to open the China trade to private interests was irresistible. In the 1830s, careful and experienced Company diplomacy, moderated by the security of the monopoly, gave way to a more forthright and aggressively commercialist policy, driven by ruthless competition. By the end of the decade, Britain and China were at war (fig. 96).

The China trade expanded massively in the early 19th century as tea became a popular beverage across all sections of British society. Tea was normally purchased with silver exported from Britain or India, but there was always a concern about this perceived drain on the nation's finances. The Company and British officials attempted to persuade the Chinese to open up their markets by accepting a greater range and quantity of manufactured goods in exchange for tea, and by removing some of the more onerous constraints on commerce. The Chinese authorities remained intransigent, disregarding the bold rhetoric of free trade; Britain now sought other means to circumvent commercial restrictions. Opium proved ideal. The drug was grown in India and smuggled to China in huge quantities in small opium clippers by numerous private traders from Britain, India and a host of other nations. It was then sold to Chinese dealers, who paid in silver; this silver was used to purchase tea for export to Britain and elsewhere.

As a solution to the trade impasse, it was perfect in every respect bar one: selling opium was illegal in China and brought the offending merchants into direct opposition with Chinese officials.

In the late 1830s, the Chinese mounted an increasingly successful campaign against opium smuggling, part of a wider drive to tackle the devastating impact of the drug on China, especially in the region around Canton. Huge volumes of opium were seized and stockpiled on the quaysides at Lintin and Canton. British merchants complained bitterly to Captain Charles Elliot of the Royal Navy, Britain's plenipotentiary at Canton, placing him under great pressure to act decisively against the Chinese. Elliot warned the foreign secretary, Lord Palmerston, that this dispute was likely to escalate and that a negotiated settlement was required. Despite his bellicose nature, Palmerston reminded Elliot in June 1838 that he was in Canton to protect and promote legitimate trade:

With respect to opium ... Her Majesty's Government cannot interfere for the purpose of enabling British subjects to violate the laws of the country to which they trade. Any loss, therefore, which such persons may suffer in consequence of more effectual execution of Chinese laws on this subject, must be borne by the parties who have brought that loss on themselves by their own acts.[2]

fig. 96
Canton from the Heights,
by Edward Cree, 1841
Canton was a bustling commercial centre and an important strategic location at the time of the First China War. It was the only place in China where European traders could procure the Chinese commodities, such as tea, that were in such huge demand in Europe and America.
[PAF6028]

Canton from the Heights
May 29. 1841

But events in Canton soon brought the affair to a head and changed attitudes in Westminster.

The key figure in China's campaign against opium was Lin Zexu. He was appointed special commissioner by the Chinese emperor to extinguish the opium trade. In March 1839, Lin demanded that all opium trading cease immediately and that all stocks of the drug be surrendered to his officials. When the European merchants refused to comply, Chinese troops surrounded the Canton factories. The Europeans were effectively held prisoner. A standoff ensued. When Elliot arrived from Macao, he too found himself detained. Realising the situation was quite hopeless, Elliot had no choice but to acquiesce in Lin's demands. He agreed that more than 20,000 cases of British opium, worth in excess of £2 million, would be handed over. Elliot, upon his own initiative, assured the merchants of his and the British government's responsibility for the value of the surrendered cases. Elliot's intervention turned the opium issue from one involving the Chinese authorities and a number of renegade traders to one implicating the two governments; this had profound repercussions. The seized contraband was duly destroyed in trenches using water and a mixture of salt and lime before being carefully poured into a stream and washed out to sea. Some 500 closely guarded labourers undertook the task, which lasted for several weeks. Lin had scored a famous, if short-lived, victory. He regarded his actions as upholding Chinese law and a fitting punishment for the smugglers; Elliot saw them as a humiliation of Britain.[3]

Further incidents followed, steadily worsening Anglo-Chinese relations at Canton and transforming the affair from an acrimonious trade disagreement to a tense, highly charged and violent dispute. News of these events took some months to reach Britain. But when it did, Palmerston acted decisively early in 1840. A substantial military and naval expedition was deployed from India to extract both the required apology and change of policy from the Chinese and the compensation necessary to meet the losses of the British opium traders. British troops and warships arrived in June 1840, representing a force that the Chinese could not hope to match in firepower or tactical discipline.

The Company was acutely interested in the events unfolding at Canton. Although the tea trade to Britain was no longer its concern, the supply of opium was of importance to the Company's government of India. Duties raised from the export of opium already

provided more than ten per cent of Indian revenues by the later 1830s. In other words, opium was becoming a significant and growing component of Company finances.[4] Company forces were therefore sent to China to bolster those of the Royal Navy. Indeed, they were further strengthened by the latest technology in the form of the steam-powered, iron-hulled vessel *Nemesis*. The new ship was built speculatively by John Laird of Birkenhead and sent as a private vessel to China. Laird appointed William Hutcheon Hall as commander (fig. 97). He was a former naval officer, who had studied steam engines in Glasgow and worked on steamboats in the United States. Undaunted by contrary winds and tides, this ship proved lethally adept in China's coastal waters and rivers in numerous actions, being attached to the Company's own naval forces. In one notable incident, the *Nemesis* encountered Admiral Kwan's fleet of 15 war junks in Anson's Bay on 7 January 1841. The action demonstrated unequivocally the technological superiority of the armed British steamers as Captain Hall employed his Congreve rockets to deadly effect (fig. 98):

fig. 98
The Hon. E. I. Co. Iron Steam Ship Nemesis, *Lieut. W. H. Hall, R.N. Commander, with Boats of [the]* Sulphur, Calliope, Larne *and* Starling Destroying the Chinese War Junks, in Anson's Bay, Jany 7th 1841, *after Edward Duncan, 1843*
In January 1841, the *Nemesis*, commanded by William Hall, destroyed a fleet of Chinese war junks. The action provided tangible evidence of the technological superiority and destructive capabilities of armed iron steamers.
[PAH8893]

Hurrah! for Canton

fig.99
Hurrah for Canton, 24 May 1841,
by Edward Cree, 1841
Edward Cree was a naval surgeon
who served with the Royal Navy
during the tumultuous events
of the First China War.

[CRE/5]

24 May 1841 E.H.C.

The very first rocket fired from the *Nemesis* was seen to enter the large junk against which it was directed, near that of the admiral, and almost instantly it blew up with a terrific explosion, launching into eternity every soul on board, and pouring forth its blaze like the mighty rush of fire from a volcano. The instantaneous destruction of the huge body seemed appalling to both sides engaged. The smoke, and flame, and thunder of the explosion, with the fragments falling round, and even portions of dissevered bodies scattering as they fell, were enough to strike with awe, if not with fear, the stoutest heart that looked upon it.[5]

Hall's account of his experiences in the *Nemesis* was influential in persuading the Navy both of the advantages of iron ships and of steam power.

Despite terrible losses like those at Anson's Bay, the imperial government in Peking, distant from the fighting, was not easily or quickly cowed into surrender. Having bombarded, seized and looted major ports like Canton, the British now struck further inland. They were able to cut vital arteries of internal trade through attacks on the Grand Canal, which severely restricted food distribution in northern China and the flow of taxes to the imperial capital. In numerous actions, China's armed forces sustained significant losses, while the British expeditionary forces suffered comparatively minor casualties.

fig.100
Ching Kiang Fou. The Last Stand of the Tartars, 21 July 1842, by Edward Cree, 1842
The Chinese sustained significant casualties during the fighting, as British firepower proved decisive and deadly. As a medical man, Cree's observations on the war are particularly poignant.
[CRE/6]

The events of the war were witnessed by Dr Edward Cree, a surgeon serving on board HMS *Rattlesnake*. His extraordinary illustrated journals record the conflict, providing unique insights into British attitudes and the impact of war on China. Cree observed an attack on Canton in 1841 (fig.99). On 24 May, he wrote:

I spent the afternoon at the mast-head, from where I could see the firing and plenty of smoke. I could see the flashes of the guns and some heavy explosions and two large fires which broke out in different parts of the city. This being the Queen's birthday the firing commenced with a royal salute of twenty-one guns from each ship at noon, soon followed by a deadlier one. Nearly all our men are away, very few left on board and no boats but the dinghy, so for safety and to prevent any attempts at boarding by gangs of Chinese robbers we had all our guns loaded with grapeshot. The night was illuminated by the flames from the city and shells and rockets flying. Our force consists of about 4000 soldiers and sailors and the Chinese have about 30,000. I stayed up most of the night watching the fires.[6]

In 1842, Cree and the *Rattlesnake* were part of the force that sailed up the Yangtze River. At Chin-Kiang-Fu he encountered the full horror and complexity of the war. The city was ravaged by a British assault and its population caught up in the resulting chaos of plunder, reprisal and bloodshed (figs 100 and 101). On 22 July, he wrote:

fig.101
Ching Kiang Fou – Burying the Killed,
by Edward Cree, 1842
Cree's illustrated journals provide an extraordinary record of the conflict, as well as a stark reminder of the brutality of the war.
[CRE/6]

Ching Kiang Foo – Burying the killed

There were shocking sights in the city, which was now almost a ruin, its ramparts and streets encumbered by the bodies of the slain, the wounded and dying, its finest buildings destroyed … beautiful shops and houses gutted by the Chinese marauders. … Frightful scenes were witnessed among the houses, whole families were slaughtered in their own homes by their own people in the streets occupied by the Tartar troops and mandarins – little children, some still breathing and writhing in agony with a broken spine or stab. In one house seven dead or dying persons were found in one room. … I was unable to leave the ship today as I had many sick and wounded to attend to. Captain Collinson, who only left us yesterday in high spirits, is amongst the killed from a shot through the heart.[7]

The following day Cree surveyed the scene ashore, estimating that some 200 British men had died, many from sunstroke, but he placed the Chinese losses at some 2,000. Before sailing for Nanking, he made a short entry in his journal on 24 July:

The city still in flames in three or four places. Empty junks and rafts continue to float down the river as well as numbers of bloated dead bodies – such are some of the horrors of war.[8]

fig.102
The Signing and Sealing of the Treaty of Nanking,
after Captain John Platt, 1846
The Treaty of Nanking, signed on 29 August 1842, brought the First China War to an end. It imposed severe terms on the Chinese, exacting compensation payments and further trading concessions. The signing ceremony took place on board HMS *Cornwallis*, a ship built by the Wadia family in Bombay.
[PAI5081]

With Shanghai and other cities now captured, Nanking open to attack and Peking blockaded, the Chinese authorities faced an impossible military position and were compelled to sue for peace. The resulting Treaty of Nanking, signed on board HMS *Cornwallis* on 29 August 1842, brought the war to a conclusion. Under its terms, the Chinese were to pay an indemnity of $21 million to compensate the opium merchants and cover the cost of Britain's punitive expedition; ports such as Canton and Shanghai were to be opened to foreign trade and settlement; and Hong Kong was acquired by Britain. Cree was clearly ambivalent about the conflict. He was in Nanking when the treaty was signed:

> So ends the Chinese war. About the justice and policy of it I leave to more competent judges, but the one thing I dislike in connection with it is the opium question. It has cost the lives of many thousands of human beings, and great destruction of property – and misery and sorrow to many.[9]

The principal cause of the conflict, opium, was not mentioned in the treaty, and the trade remained illegal. But the victory was seen as an important step in bringing China and its vast potential markets within the reach of Britain's global economy (figs 102 and 103).

fig.103
Medal commemorating the end of the war with China, 1842
This medal, with its inscription 'The Triumph of British Arms', celebrates Britain's victory in the First China War. Under the terms of the Treaty of Nanking, China had to pay compensation, open up further ports to foreign trade and transfer control of Hong Kong to Britain.

[MEC1104]

Taking full advantage of the new opportunities provided by the treaty proved rather difficult. Relations between Britain and China remained tense in the treaty ports during the 1840s and early 1850s as both sides tried to adapt to changed circumstances: the British anxious to press home their advantage and the Chinese determined to yield as little as possible. There were frequent small-scale disputes and occasional clashes between the Chinese and local British forces over a host of misunderstandings and apparent insults, particularly in and around Canton and the developing colony of Hong Kong.

There were, however, areas of co-operation between the two countries. Both had a genuine interest in the suppression of piracy, which was widespread and highly disruptive. Britain was keen to eradicate the menace to protect and stimulate its trade; China wanted to maximise its tax and customs revenues through the promotion of legitimate commerce. Dr Cree, still with the Navy in eastern waters after a furlough in Edinburgh to complete his medical training, was involved in a number of joint Anglo-Chinese anti-piracy patrols. In 1849, he witnessed two significant encounters in quick succession, indicating the scale and ferocity of these operations. On 1 October, his ship, HMS *Fury*, attacked the pirate squadron of Chui-apoo. The pirate junks sustained their fire against the *Fury* and other British vessels but were soon overwhelmed, as Cree noted (fig.104):

The firing of shot, shell and grape was too hot for the rascals and all the junks were in a blaze, and as many of the pirates as were able were swarming over the sides and swimming to the shore. Twenty-seven junks with a number of small vessels were destroyed. It is supposed that 400 of the pirates perished and the rest, upwards of 1,000 escaped to the shore.

Cree recorded the next day that Chui-apoo was 'desperately wounded' but had made it to land. Only a few days later the *Fury* was again hunting pirates, this time the fleet of the 'desperate robber' Shap-'ng-tsai (fig.105).[10] General Wang, a naval mandarin, commanded a Chinese squadron that sailed with the British in pursuit of the renegades. Once more the encounter with the pirate fleet was bloody and swiftly executed. Those pirates who managed to escape their junks were, in this case, attacked as they reached the shore by enraged locals, who had long suffered from Shap-'ng-tsai's reign of terror. Cree observed the joint action:

Our old General, Wang, showed some pluck in jumping overboard from one of the boats and swimming to a junk and capturing three of the pirates himself. They were so frightened at seeing one of their mandarins that they made no resistance.

The impact of such actions was immediate. Dr Cree reported at the end of the engagement that some 58 junks were destroyed and perhaps more than 2,000 pirates and their unfortunate captives were killed. The British and

fig.104
Destruction of Chui-apoo's Pirate Fleet, 30 September 1849, **by Nam-Sing, c.1850**
Piracy presented a major commercial problem for both China and Britain in the South China Seas. In 1849, a fleet of pirate junks was destroyed in a joint action by an Anglo-Chinese squadron. This painting was commissioned by Dugald McEwan, assistant surgeon of HMS *Hastings*.
[BHC0632]

fig. 105

Flag, 19th century

This flag was a shrine hanging in one of Shap 'ng-tsai's pirate junks. It depicts one of the four Emperors of Heaven. He is seated on a mythical beast with a pillar behind him. The bats along the side are a punning reference to good luck.

[AAA0554]

聖母 天后

Chinese celebrated their success with reciprocal receptions on shore and aboard the *Fury*.[11] But this form of easy co-operation was the exception.

In 1856, Britain and China again lurched into war. Chinese officials in Canton arrested the crew of the *Arrow*, a Chinese ship with a lapsed British registration, on suspicion of piracy. It was alleged that the *Arrow* was flying a British ensign and, therefore, China's actions had insulted the flag. Once more, a minor local incident escalated to provide the spark for conflict, which involved Britain in alliance with France, Russia and the United States. The war began in earnest with a British attack on Canton. Ferocious fighting at Fatshan Creek in June 1857, for example, saw a British force, largely in open boats, take and narrowly defeat a large number of war junks under the command of General Wang. The Chinese, having learned a good deal from earlier encounters and their co-operation with the Royal Navy, put up a formidable and disciplined defence. In fact, British operations against Canton, although individually successful, lacked the strength of numbers necessary to occupy the city effectively, particularly given the open hostility of the Cantonese towards westerners.[12] The outbreak of the Indian Mutiny in May 1857 further compounded the lack of resources. It took until early 1858 for Anglo-French forces to achieve their objective of occupying Canton. Further assaults compelled the Chinese, who were simultaneously dealing with the massive Taiping rebellion that cost millions of lives, to seek a settlement. The Treaty of Tientsin was signed on 28 June 1858, which gave Britain and its allies access to more ports and the Chinese interior, as well as yielding a host of other privileges, including the right to have a legation in Peking. It also legalised the opium trade (figs 106 and 107).[13]

In Peking, however, hawks at the imperial court persuaded the Chinese emperor to repudiate the treaty. China and the western allies returned to conflict. In 1860, with India secure, a force of 11,000 British troops and nearly 7,000 French marched on Peking, entering the city on 6 October having annihilated the Chinese army. The emperor fled. Lord Elgin, the British plenipotentiary, ordered the burning of the already-looted Summer Palaces. Humiliated, the Chinese authorities conceded defeat and ratified the Treaty of Tientsin in the Convention of Peking on 18 October 1860.[14] The Second China War was over, and a series of 'unequal treaties' established a pattern of Anglo-Chinese relations that was to survive until well into the twentieth century.

fig.106
Cannon ball, 19th century
The inscription on this object recounts its remarkable history: 'Shot fired from the North Wong Tong Chinese fort at the mouth of the Canton River. The shot entered the foremost part of the port side of HMS *"Mankin"* cutting a boy in two.' HMS *Nankin*, misspelled on the inscription, took part in the Second China War.

[KTP1070]

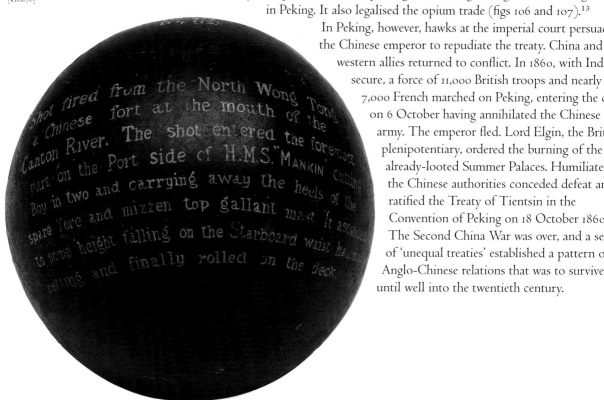

fig.107
Imperial Chinese flag, c.1857
This flag was acquired by Robert
John Le Mesurier McClure during
the capture of Canton in the Second
China War. McClure led one of
three divisions of the British naval
brigade. On 29 December 1857,
French and British troops stormed
the city by scaling its walls.

[AAA0559]

THE INDIAN MUTINY
AND THE END OF THE COMPANY

Through the 18th and early 19th centuries, the East India Company came under great public scrutiny and increasing British government control. Criticisms of its long-standing commercial monopolies and the controversies surrounding its control and exploitation of large tracts of the subcontinent raised questions about the future existence of the Company. These pressures at home were also to be matched by new challenges in India, which eventually led to the Company's abolition in 1858.

The origins of the Indian Mutiny and the associated popular uprising across much of northern India are complex and controversial. In essence, they are related to the changing nature of Company rule in India. The aggressive expansion of the Company Raj was accompanied by government intervention in a much wider range of Indian affairs, from religion and traditional customs to education and law. New technologies like the telegraph and the railway were introduced, which further disrupted the established social order. The combination of factors was bewildering: pressure from Christian missionaries and fears of mass conversions; the pace and scope of military reform; the annexation of yet more territory; harsher racial attitudes among the new generation of military officers and Company administrators; and simmering local resentments against a slew of issues little understood or recognised by the Company. To this potent powder keg was added the seemingly unstoppable rumour of pork and beef fat being used to grease the cartridges for the new Enfield rifles issued to the Company's armies. This apparent disregard for the religious beliefs of both its Hindu and its Muslim sepoys seemed to characterise the Company's increasingly remote and insensitive rule.

A vicious conflagration was ignited. Unable to contain a mutiny by troops in the Bengal Army at Meerut in April 1857, the Company lost control over a large swathe of northern India as its authority unravelled amid insurrection and popular revolt. The result was an appalling and murderous horror as rebels slaughtered Europeans and loyal Indians indiscriminately. As news reached Britain, the public, disgusted by the events at Cawnpore and elsewhere, demanded swift and wrathful revenge. There was also universal criticism of Company rule and immediate demands for a wholesale change in the government of India. British retribution was equally as bloody, with mutineers hanged, blown from cannon and made to suffer untold degradations. Efforts to regain control of India took until the summer of 1858 (fig.108).

While the campaign was principally military in nature, it involved a significant and sometimes surprising use of naval and maritime resources.

fig.109
Captain William Peel,
by John Lucas, 1859–60
William Peel, the third son
of Sir Robert Peel, joined the
Royal Navy at the age of 14.
He saw action around the
world, before leading a naval
brigade during the Indian
Mutiny. He was severely
wounded in action and died
at Cawnpore in 1858. This
portrait was commissioned by
public subscription. The Lords
Commissioners of the
Admiralty ordered it to be
placed in the Painted Hall at
Greenwich in 1860.

[BHC2943]

Specially contracted ships and naval vessels transported thousands of troops to India in 1857 to crush the mutiny and the associated civil insurrection. Regiments were deployed from across the British Empire; the Royal Navy sent men ashore too, with marines and naval brigades fighting far inland. Both typical and exemplary of the Navy's involvement were the actions of Captain Sir William Peel (figs 109 and 110). Peel was an early Victorian popular hero *par excellence*. The bright and resourceful third son of the Tory prime minister Sir Robert Peel, he entered the Navy in 1838. Although his rapid progression through the ranks was undoubtedly eased by family and political connections, it was driven by his talent and aptitude. Peel saw action off the coast of Syria in 1840, was involved in secret intelligence missions in the Americas, journeyed up the Nile and explored the Sudanese desert, and was awarded the Victoria Cross for his repeated displays of conspicuous bravery during the Crimean War (1854–56). At the outbreak of the Second China War (1856–60), Peel was in command of the steam frigate HMS *Shannon*. At Singapore in June 1857, while en route to Hong Kong, news reached the ship of the outbreak of the Indian Mutiny. Upon his return from China, Peel formed a 450-strong naval brigade at Calcutta with sailors, marines and soldiers from the *Shannon*. Armed with six 24-pounder artillery guns and two 8-inch howitzers, the brigade fought at Allahabad, providing formidable firepower under Peel's cool and efficient direction. Further

fig. 110
European Sailors of the Indian Navy, Breaching the Delhi Gate, 1858, engraved by A. Maclure
A number of naval brigades were involved in suppressing the rebellion in India. The sailors brought heavy artillery ashore, travelled far inland and engaged in fierce fighting. In August 1857, HMS *Shannon* arrived in India. Commanded by William Peel, its crew formed a 'naval brigade' of over 450 men.

[PAD5908]

engagements followed. He deployed six of the ship's massive 8-inch guns, mounting them on carriages constructed by the sailors. This reinforcement turned Peel's naval brigade into an effective, heavily armed field force. On 9 March 1858 at Lucknow, Peel was shot in the thigh and very severely wounded; the bullet was dug out of the other side of his leg. Weakened by his injuries, he succumbed to smallpox at Cawnpore and died there on 27 April. He was 33 years old.

Other members of Peel's naval brigade distinguished themselves at Lucknow. The action at the Shah Najaf mosque on 17 November 1857 was particularly fraught and brought the brigade the honour of a number of Victoria Crosses. Lieutenant Nowell Salmon and Leading Seaman John Harrison of the *Shannon* and a Lieutenant Southwell volunteered to climb a tree near the mosque to survey the situation. Southwell was killed at once, but Salmon and Harrison, despite withering fire and being wounded, were able to report on the enemy's position. Both received the VC. On the same day, Lieutenant Thomas Young and Able Seaman George Hall were also involved in acts of extraordinary bravery in the deadly attempt to breach the walls of the mosque. Hall explained:

After firing each round we ran our gun forward, until at last my gun's crew were actually in danger of being hit by splinters of brick and stone mortar from the walls we were bombarding. Our Lieutenant, Mr Thomas Young, moved about with a quiet smile and a word of encouragement, and when at last the gunner next to me fell dead, Mr Young at once took his place.[15]

Hall, 'a man remarkable for his steady good conduct and his athletic frame', was a Canadian, the son of freed American slaves, and the first black man to be awarded the Victoria Cross. Young, of whom it was said 'the heavier the fire he was under, the cooler and steadier did he become', also gained the award.[16] Before the men of the naval brigade were to embark for home in the *Shannon*, they were honoured with parades and receptions in Calcutta. The advocate-general toasted the brigade and concluded:

Nobly you have sustained the honour of the Union Jack in regions to which sailors have never carried it before. To our great regret, the *Shannon* is about to leave Calcutta, and wherever she goes she will carry with her our heartfelt good wishes, our blessings and our prayers. You will leave behind you the memory of your gallant deeds, your endurance, discipline and good conduct. We know that the memory of Sir William Peel will never be forgotten by that gallant crew whom he taught, as Nelson did his sailors and Wellington his soldiers, to go anywhere and do anything.[17]

The *Shannon* sailed on 15 September and reached Spithead on 29 December 1858.

By this time, the new Government of India Act had abolished the East India Company (fig.111), as Antony Wild explains with an alphabetical flourish:

The India Bill was passed on 2 August 1858, and the Company's remaining armies, batteries, churches, colleges, debts, desks, elephants, godowns, graves, judges, lascars, navies, paintings, papers, pensioners, prisoners, powers, treaties, territories, vassals, vessels, warehouses and whorehouses were vested in Her Majesty Queen Victoria.[10]

The Crown, through Parliament and a secretary of state, now ruled India. Queen Victoria issued a proclamation announcing the change to her millions of new Indian subjects on 1 November 1858. She pledged that the new government would treat all its subjects equally, respect India's religions, defend the rights of the princes and thereby maintain the social order. India was now, formally, part of the British Empire and the brightest jewel in Victoria's burgeoning imperial diadem.

The East India Company's grand headquarters in Leadenhall Street were demolished in the 1860s, and what had once been the most powerful commercial organisation in the world and an Asian power of considerable might slowly passed out of the national consciousness. Its inglorious and ignoble collapse obscured both its astonishing longevity and its undeniable past glories.

EXECUTION OF "JOHN COMPANY;"
The Blowing up (there ought to be) in Leadenhall Street.

fig. 111
Execution of 'John Company':
The blowing up [there ought to be] in
Leadenhall Street, **by John Leech,**
***Punch,* 15 August 1857**
The Indian Mutiny convinced the British government that a trading company could not be left in charge of a vast territorial empire. The East India Company was abolished in 1858 and responsibility for governing India passed to Westminster.
[Punch Ltd]

fig. 112 *(overleaf)*
Shipping off Canton,
Chinese school, c.1850
This bustling river scene shows small local junks and larger trading vessels. In the centre of the painting is a steamship. Vessels like this were responsible for finally breaking the monsoon system, which had defined the East India Company's maritime trading world.
[BHC1777]

THE COMPANY, ITS DEMISE AND ITS LEGACIES, C.1830–70

TECHNOLOGY AND THE END OF BRITAIN'S
MONSOON TRADE

The technological advances of the 19th century had a profound impact on Britain's continuing maritime engagement with Asia. Ship design, new forms of propulsion, and the opening of the Suez Canal all signalled key changes in the operations of Britain's maritime system in the East, which affected trade, government and the projection of British power across the Indian Ocean world (fig. 112).

The development of faster sailing ships and the gradual introduction of steam power helped to transform communications between Europe and Asia. In the middle of the 19th century, slender-hulled clipper ships – like the famous *Cutty Sark* (1869), a late example – were employed in the tea trade, sailing swiftly back to Britain with the first crop, which commanded the highest price on the London market. In 1866, a great race between the leading clipper ships of the day resulted in China tea reaching the London docks via the Cape, a voyage of 14,000 miles, in only 99 days, significantly quicker than even the fastest East Indiaman. The first three ships – the *Taeping*, the *Ariel* and the *Serica* – arrived within two hours of each other, carrying a combined cargo of nearly 3.3 million pounds of tea. The *Taeping* gained the premium of an extra ten shillings per ton for its tea.[19]

It was the steamship, however, that truly revolutionised Britain's trade with Asia. No longer wholly reliant on tides, currents and favourable winds, steamships finally broke free of the seasonal monsoon system that had determined the cycle of Indian Ocean trade for millennia. Voyages were timetabled. Improvements in steam technology increased both the speed and the size of vessels, introducing economies of scale through the volume of goods that could be carried and the efficiencies resulting from more frequent, reliable voyages. But further changes affected even the route to Asia. In 1869, the same year as the launch of the *Cutty Sark*, the vessel that marked the apogee of the clipper ship, the Suez Canal opened. The canal altered the pattern of Europe's trade in the Indian Ocean forever, truly marking the end of its involvement in, and reliance on, the old monsoon trading system. The canal, which cut the distance between Britain and India by at least 4,500 miles, was exclusively for the use of steamships. Sailing ships could not exploit this massive short-cut and were thus compelled to use the longer Cape route. Gradually, as the 19th century advanced, the competitive edge of sail diminished: the Suez Canal became the steam highway of empire and 'east of Suez' the shorthand for Britain's sprawling imperial possessions across the old trading world of the Honourable Company.

CONCLUSIONS

Throughout the more than 250 years of its existence, the East India Company was a maritime concern. Its fortunes were dependent on the maintenance of regular and uninterrupted sailings to and from Asia. The Company's great fleets of East Indiamen not only carried the cargoes of Asian goods that were the basis of its long commercial success, but also transported the bullion, personnel, intelligence, stores, equipment and military hardware necessary to pursue trading profit and to carve out and administer a vast, populous empire. The need to secure these long chains of communication and supply was paramount and essentially unchanging. The Company employed its own navy, the Bombay Marine, to defend the sea routes, and entered into a mutually supportive relationship with the Royal Navy in the East. Challenges to its maritime security from Asian and European rivals were, on the whole, successfully repulsed.

The Company exerted a unique and lasting influence on both Britain and Asia. The Company's enormous trading success helped to transform British commerce and the wider economy. Its complex patterns of trade stimulated the growth of the financial infrastructure of the City of London. The Company's projection of power in Asia laid the foundations of much of the Victorian empire. Its impact on Asia, and India in particular, was undeniably far less positive. But the long history of the Company and its maritime world now seem to resonate with growing contemporary concerns over multinational businesses and the rapacious effects of globalisation. More than a century and a half after its demise, the East India Company appears relevant again.

Notes

Introduction (pages 12–21)

1 'The East India House', *Illustrated London News*, 3 August 1861, 125.

2 Thomas Babington Macaulay, 'A Speech Delivered in the House of Commons on the 10th of July, 1833', in Barbara Harlow and Mia Carter (eds), *Archives of Empire, Volume 1: From the East India Company to the Suez Canal* (London: Duke University Press, 2003), 54, 57.

3 Quoted in Jean Sutton, *Lords of the East: The East India Company and its Ships, 1600–1874* (London: Conway Maritime Press, 2000), 40.

4 Quoted in Denis Judd, *The Lion and the Tiger: The Rise and Fall of the British Raj, 1600–1947* (Oxford: Oxford University Press, 2005), 2.

5 Ibid., 4.

6 Quoted in Sir Evan Cotton with Sir Charles Fawcett, *East Indiamen: The East India Company's Maritime Service* (London: The Batchwood Press, 1949), 11.

7 Clements R. Markham (ed.), *The Voyages of Sir James Lancaster, Kt., to the East Indies, with Abstracts of Journals of Voyages to the East Indies during the Seventeenth Century, Preserved in the India Office* (London: The Hakluyt Society, 1877), 59, 62.

8 'Instructions Given by the Governor and Committee of the Company of Merchants Trading to the East Indies to Lawrence Femell, the Principal Factor, and the Other Factors Employed in the Sixth Voyage', in Markham (ed.), *Voyages of Sir James Lancaster*, 131.

9 Ibid., 132–135.

10 Ibid., 137–144.

Chapter 1 (pages 22–57)

1 Adam Smith, *An Enquiry into the Nature and Causes of the Wealth of Nations* [1776], 2 vols (London: Routledge, 1905), vol. 2, 139.

2 Quoted in Kenneth Macpherson, *The Indian Ocean: A History of People and the Sea* (Oxford: Oxford University Press, 1993), 79.

3 Quoted in Michael Pearson, *The Indian Ocean* (London: Routledge, 2003), 83.

4 Quoted in William Foster, *England's Quest of Eastern Trade* (London: A. & C. Black, 1933), 147.

5 These figures are taken from K. N. Chaudhuri, *The English East India Company: The Study of an Early Joint-Stock Company, 1600–1640* (London: Frank Cass, 1965), 22. Chaudhuri's study contains a wealth of detailed information on the establishment and early years of the Company.

6 Figures on the Company's trade are taken from K. N. Chaudhuri, *The Trading World of Asia and the English East India Company, 1660–1760* (Cambridge: Cambridge University Press, 1978), *passim*.

7 John Cary, quoted in John E. Wills, Jr, 'European Consumption and Asian Production', in John Brewer and Roy Porter (eds), *Consumption and the World of Goods* (London: Routledge, 1993), 136.

Chapter 2 (pages 58–89)

1 'Voyage of Thomas Cavendish round the Whole Earth', in Richard Hakluyt, *Voyages and Discoveries: The Principal Navigations, Voyages, Traffiques and Discoveries of the English Nation*, ed. Jack Beeching (Harmondsworth: Penguin, 1972), 294.

2 'Voyage of Francis Drake about the Whole Globe', in Hakluyt, *Voyages and Discoveries*, 183–186.

3 Thomas Roe to George Abbot, Lord Archbishop of Canterbury, 29 January 1616, in William Foster (ed.), *The Embassy of Sir Thomas Roe to the Court of the Great Mogul, 1615–1619*, 2 vols (London: The Hakluyt Society, 1899), vol. 1, 122.

4 Ibid., 123.

5 Basil Lubbock (ed.), *Barlow's Journal of his Life at Sea in King's Ships, East & West Indiamen & other Merchantmen from 1659 to 1703*, 2 vols (London: Hurst & Blackett, 1934), vol. 1, 278.

6 'Voyage of Francis Drake', 187.

7 Samuel Purchas, *Hakluytus Posthumus, or Purchas his Pilgrimes*, 20 vols (Glasgow: James MacLehose, 1905), vol. 2, 349.

8 Rowland Raven-Hart (ed.), *Before Van Riebeeck: Callers at South Africa from 1488 to 1652* (Cape Town: Struik, 1967), 47.

9 Foster (ed.), *Embassy of Sir Thomas Roe*, vol. 1, 11–12.

10 Lubbock (ed.), *Barlow's Journal*, vol. 1, 239.

11 'Voyage of Ralph Fitch to Goa and Siam', in Hakluyt, *Voyages and Discoveries*, 256.

12 William Biddulph to Sir Thomas Smythe, 28 October 1613, in Frederick Danvers and William Foster (eds), *Letters Received by the East India Company from its Servants in the East*, 6 vols (London: Sampson Low, Marston and Co., 1896–1902), vol. 1, 301.

13 Clements R. Markham (ed.), *The Voyages of Sir James Lancaster, Kt., to the East Indies, with Abstracts of Journals of Voyages to the East Indies during the Seventeenth Century, Preserved in the India Office* (London: The Hakluyt Society, 1877), 71, 100.

14 British Library (BL), Asia, Pacific and Africa Collections (APAC), East India Company Factory Records, IOR/G/40/10/126–127.

15 William Foster, 'An English Settlement in Madagascar', *English Historical Review*, 27:106 (1912), 245, 248.

16 Thomas Roe to Henry Wriothesley, Earl of Southampton, 14 February 1615, in Foster (ed.), *Embassy of Sir Thomas Roe*, vol. 1, 134.

17 Quoted in Harihar Das, *The Norris Embassy to Aurangzib, 1699–1702*, ed. S. C. Sarkar (Calcutta: K. L. Mukhopadhyay, 1959), 149.

18 Lubbock (ed.), *Barlow's Journal*, vol. 1, 185, 190; vol. 2, 363.

19 Ibid., vol. 1, 221–222.

20 Jean-Baptiste Du Halde, *A Description of the Empire of China and Chinese-Tartary*, 2 vols (London: Edward Cave, 1738–41), vol. 1, 279, 280.

21 H. B. Morse, *Chronicles of the East India Company Trading to China, 1635–1834*, 5 vols (Oxford: Clarendon Press, 1926), vol. 1, 98.

22 Thomas Roe to Lord Carew, 17 January 1616, in Foster (ed.), *Embassy of Sir Thomas Roe*, vol. 1, 111.

23 Purchas, *Hakluytus Posthumus*, vol. 3, 30, 31–33, 36.

24 Foster (ed.), *Embassy of Sir Thomas Roe*, vol. 1, 226.

25 Amin Jaffer, 'Diplomatic Encounters: Europe and South Asia', in Anna Jackson and Amin Jaffer (eds), *Encounters: The Meeting of Asia and Europe, 1500–1800* (London: V&A Publications, 2004), 77.

26 Michael Strachan, 'Terry, Edward (1589/90–1660)', *Oxford Dictionary of National Biography*, 60 vols (Oxford: Oxford University Press, 2004), vol. 54, 165.

27 For the story of the embassy, see William Foster, *John Company* (London: The Bodley Head, 1926), 97–120.

28 See, for example, the letter sent by Nathaniel Foxcroft to Robert Boyle from Fort St George on 11 September 1666, in Michael Hunter, Antonio Clericuzio and Lawrence M. Principe (eds), *The Correspondence of Robert Boyle: Volume 3, 1666–7* (London: Pickering & Chatto, 2001), 221–234.

29 Markham (ed.), *Voyages of Sir James Lancaster*, 97.

30 Ibid., 136, 144.

31 John Chamberlain to Sir Dudley Carleton, in Foster (ed.), *Embassy of Sir Thomas Roe*, vol.2, 521.

32 Foster, *John Company*, 85–92.

33 Lubbock (ed.), *Barlow's Journal*, vol.1, 194.

34 Markham (ed.), *Voyages of Sir James Lancaster*, 132–134, 164.

35 Ibid., iii, 77.

36 Quoted in Sanjay Subrahmanyam, 'Frank Submissions: The Company and the Mughals between Sir Thomas Roe and Sir William Norris', in H. V. Bowen, Margarette Lincoln and Nigel Rigby (eds) *The Worlds of the East India Company* (Woodbridge: Boydell, 2003), 72.

37 Quoted in Foster (ed.), *Embassy of Sir Thomas Roe*, vol.1, iii.

38 Quoted in Michael Strachan, *Sir Thomas Roe, 1581–1644* (Salisbury: Michael Russell, 1989), 79, 101, 145.

39 Markham (ed.), *Voyages of Sir James Lancaster*, 133.

40 Foster (ed.), *Embassy of Sir Thomas Roe*, vol.1, 146–147.

41 Quoted in Subrahmanyam, 'Frank Submissions', 73.

42 Thomas Roe to directors of the East India Company, 24 November 1616, in Foster (ed.), *Embassy of Sir Thomas Roe*, vol.2, 344.

43 Strachan, *Sir Thomas Roe*, 114, 117.

44 Robert Knox, *An Historical Relation of Ceylon* (Glasgow: James MacLehose, 1911), 193.

45 Richard Walter, *A Voyage Round the World in the Years MDCCXL, I, II, III, IV by George Anson* (London: Knapton, 1748), 536.

46 Ibid, 541.

47 BL, Add. MS 35174, fo 34v, William Alexander, 'Journal of a Voyage to Pekin in China onboard the Hindostan EIM which accompanied Lord Macartney on his Embassy to the Emperor'.

48 National Maritime Museum (NMM), HSR/N/9 [1817], fo 5.

49 Quoted in P. J. Marshall, 'Britain and China in the Late Eighteenth Century', in Robert Bickers (ed.), *Ritual and Diplomacy: The Macartney Mission to China, 1792–1794* (London: British Association for Chinese Studies, 1993), 15–16.

50 BL, APAC, IOR/G/12/92/545–86, 'An Account of Sundry Articles Purchased by Francis Baring Esq., Chairman … Consigned to the Care of Lord Viscount Macartney'.

51 Maxine Berg, 'Britain, Industry and Perceptions of China: Matthew Boulton, "Useful Knowledge" and the Macartney Embassy of 1792–4', *Journal of Global History*, 1 (2006), 275.

52 Quoted in Marshall, 'Britain and China', 14.

53 J. L. Cranmer-Byng (ed.), *An Embassy to China: Lord Macartney's Journal, 1793–1794* (London: Longmans, 1962), 74, 124.

54 J. L. Cranmer-Byng, 'China, 1792–94', in Peter Roebuck (ed.), *Macartney of Lisanoure, 1737–1806* (Belfast: Ulster Historical Foundation, 1983), 228.

55 Zhang Shunhong, 'Historical Anachronism: The Qing Court's Perception of and Reaction to the Macartney Embassy', in Bickers (ed.), *Ritual and Diplomacy*, 41.

56 James L. Hevia, 'Diplomatic Encounters: Europe and East Asia', in Jackson and Jaffer (eds), *Encounters*, 95–96.

57 Quoted in Marshall, 'Britain and China', 22–23.

58 Quoted in Cranmer-Byng, 'China', 239.

59 NMM, HSR/N/9 [1817], fos 1, 2.

60 Cranmer-Byng (ed.), *Embassy to China*, 219.

61 Edmund Burke [to William Robertson], 9 June 1777, quoted in F. P. Lock, *Edmund Burke: Volume 1, 1730–1784* (Oxford: Clarendon Press, 2008), 136.

Chapter 3 (pages 90–125)

1 David Macpherson, *Annals of Commerce, Manufactures, Fisheries, and Navigation with Brief Notices of the Arts and Sciences Connected with Them*, 4 vols (London: Nichols and Son, 1805), frontispiece.

2 *Monthly Review*, vol.46 (1772), 236.

3 *The Speech of Mr Joseph Hume at the East India House on the 6th October 1813…* (London: Cox and Baylis, 1813), 10.

4. Much useful information on East India House and the history of the Company in London is to be found in William Foster, *The East India House: Its History and Associations* (London: John Lane, 1924)

and idem, *John Company* (London: The Bodley Head, 1926).

5 Quoted in Foster, *East India House*, 133.

6 British Library (BL), Asia, Pacific and Africa Collections (APAC), India Office Records (IOR), H/763 (a), 'The Description and Dimensions of the New Front to the East India House, Leadenhall Street, by Richard Jupp, esq., Architect and Messrs. D. Pinder and W. Norris, Masons', 21.

7 Charles Stewart, *Travels of Mirza Abu Taleb Khan in Asia, Africa, and Europe during the Years 1799, 1800, 1801, 1802, and 1803*, 3 vols (London: Longman, 1814), vol.1, 84–85.

8 For the furnishings and internal decoration of East India House during the 18th century see Mildred Archer, *The India Office Collection of Paintings and Sculpture* (London: British Library, 1986) and John Hardy, *India Office Furniture* (London: British Library, 1982).

9 For a map of 1806 indicating the location of the Company's London properties see BL, IOR/H/763, 7–8.

10 Edward Brayley Wedlake et al., *A Topographical and Historical Description of London and Middlesex*, 5 vols (London: Sherwood, Neely and Jones, 1814), vol.2, 774–775.

11 Quoted in George Tierney, *The Real Situation of the East India Company Considered* (London: J. Debrett, 1787), 9.

12 *Fourth Report from the [House of Commons] Select Committee on the Affairs of the East India Company* (1812), 418.

13 *Parliamentary Papers* (1812–13), vol.8, 76.

14 Quoted in C. Northcote Parkinson, *Trade in the Eastern Seas, 1793–1813* (Cambridge: Cambridge University Press, 1937), 288.

15 Quoted in Stephen Taylor, *Storm and Conquest: The Battle for the Indian Ocean, 1809* (London: Faber and Faber, 2007), 57.

16 West Glamorgan Archive Service, SL/19, vol.3.

17 Peter Quennell (ed.), *Memoirs of William Hickey* (London: Hutchinson, 1960), 104–105.

18 Quoted in Stephen Taylor, *Caliban's Shore: The Wreck of the Grosvenor and the Strange Fate of Her Survivors* (New York and London: W. W. Norton & Co., 2004), 52.

19 Quennell (ed.), *Memoirs of William Hickey*, 108.

20 Mary, Lady Nugent, *A Journal From the Year 1811 Till the Year 1815, Including a Voyage to and Residence in India…*, 2 vols (London: n. p., 1839), vol.1, 28, 35.

Chapter 4 (pages 126–157)

1 'The Voyage of Captain Sharpeigh, 1608–1609. Being the Fourth Voyage Set Forth by the East India Company', in Clements R. Markham (ed.), *The Voyages of Sir James Lancaster, Kt., to the East Indies, with Abstracts of Journals of Voyages to the East Indies during the Seventeenth Century, Preserved in the India Office* (London: The Hakluyt Society, 1877), 121.

2 'A Court of Sales and a General Court', 30 October 1640 (Court Book, vol.17, 327), in Ethel B. Sainsbury, *A Calendar of Court Minutes, etc. of the East India Company, 1640–1643* (Oxford: Clarendon Press, 1907–38), 106, 107.

3 'The First Voyage Made to East India by Master James Lancaster for the Merchants of London, Anno 1600', in Markham (ed.), *Voyages of Sir James Lancaster*, 74.

4 Jean Sutton, *Lords of the East: The East India Company and its Ships, 1600–1874* (London: Conway Maritime Press, 2000), 80.

5 C. F. Beckingham, 'Lancaster, Sir James (1554/5–1618)', *Oxford Dictionary of National Biography*, 60 vols (Oxford: Oxford University Press, 2004), vol.32, 358.

6 'The Voyage of Captain Sharpeigh', 130.

7 'Instructions Given to … Lawrence Femell', in Markham (ed.), *Voyages of Sir James Lancaster*, 134.

8 'Journal of Ralph Crosse, Purser of the *Hosiander* in the Tenth Voyage. AD 1612', in Markham (ed.), *Voyages of Sir James Lancaster*, 234–235.

9 Basil Lubbock (ed.), *Barlow's Journal of his Life at Sea in King's Ships, East & West Indiamen & other Merchantmen from 1659 to 1703*, 2 vols (London: Hurst & Blackett, 1934), vol.1, 232.

10 William Foster (ed.), *The Embassy of Sir Thomas Roe to the Court of the Great Mogul, 1615–1619*, 2 vols (London: The Hakluyt Society, 1899), vol.1, 228.

11 C. R. Boxer, 'The Third Anglo-Dutch War in the East', *Mariner's Mirror*, 16 (1930), 371–372.

12 Lubbock (ed.), *Barlow's Journal*, vol.1, 226–234.

13 Robert Knox, *An Historical Relation of Ceylon* (Glasgow: James MacLehose, 1911), 91.

14 Charles Rathbone Low, *History of the Indian Navy (1613–1863)*, 2 vols (London: Richard Bentley and Son, 1877), vol.1, 81.

15 Lubbock (ed.), *Barlow's Journal*, vol.2, 473.

16 British Library (BL), Asia, Pacific and Africa Collections (APAC), East India Company Minutes and Memoranda of General Committees, IOR/D/93/451–452, 21 August 1713.

17 BL, APAC, East India Company Minutes of the Court of Directors and Court of Proprietors, IOR/B/56/42, 17 June 1720.

18 BL, APAC, East India Company Minutes and Memoranda of General Committees, IOR/D/97 (no fos), 22 June 1720.

19 Low, *History of the Indian Navy*, vol.1, 90–91.

20 BL, APAC, East India Company Minutes of the Court of Directors and Court of Proprietors, IOR/B/77/304, 19 February 1762.

21 Quoted in Sutton, *Lords of the East*, 81.

22 Quoted in C. Northcote Parkinson, *War in the Eastern Seas, 1793–1815* (London: George Allen & Unwin, 1954), 194.

23 Sutton, *Lords of the East*, 111.

24 National Maritime Museum (NMM), HMN/38, 'Proceedings of an Especial Meeting of the Society of East India Commanders', 22 August 1804, 4.

25 *Naval Chronicle*, vol.12 (1804), 345–349; quoted in Sutton, *Lords of the East*, 115.

26 NMM, HMN/38, 'Proceedings of a General Meeting of the Committee for Managing the Patriotic Fund', 14 August 1804.

27 NMM, HMN/38, 'Proceedings of an Especial Meeting of the Society of East India Commanders', 22 August 1804, 5.

28 NMM, HMN/38, 'Proceedings of a General Meeting of the Committee for Managing the Patriotic Fund', 14 August 1804.

29 NMM, ADL/P/16/1, William Ramsey to William Marsden, 18 August 1804.

30 John Blankett to Evan Nepean, 25 January 1795, in George McCall Theal, *Records of the Cape Colony*, 36 vols (Cape Town: Official Publications, 1897–1905), vol.1, 26.

31 Parkinson, *War in the Eastern Seas*, 412.

32 Ibid., 417.

33 Quoted in Susan Stronge, *Tipu's Tigers* (London: V&A Publications, 2009), 14.

34 Ibid., 32.

Chapter 5 (pages 158–185)

1 'Government of India Act, 1833', in Barbara Harlow and Mia Carter (eds), *Archives of Empire, Volume 1: From the East India Company to the Suez Canal* (Durham, NC: Duke University Press, 2003), 49.

2 Palmerston to Elliot, 15 June 1838, quoted in Glenn Melancon, 'Honour in Opium? The British Declaration of War on China, 1839–1840', *International History Review*, 21:4 (1999), 859.

3 Hsin-pao Chang, *Commissioner Lin and the Opium War* (Cambridge, MA: Harvard University Press, 1964), 160–179.

4 J. Y. Wong, *Deadly Dreams: Opium, Imperialism and the Arrow War (1856–1860) in China* (Cambridge: Cambridge University Press, 1998), 397–398.

5 W. D. Bernard, *The Nemesis in China, Comprising a History of the Late War in that Country … from the Notes of Captain W. H. Hall, RN* (3rd edn, London: Henry Colburn, 1847), 91.

6 E. H. Cree, *The Cree Journals: The Voyages of Edward H. Cree, Surgeon R.N., as Related in his Private Journals, 1837–1856*, ed. Michael Levien (Exeter: Webb & Bower, 1981), 80–81.

7 Ibid., 104–105.

8 Ibid., 106.

9 Ibid., 117.

10 Ibid., 193.

11 Ibid., 197–204.

12 Gerald S. Graham, *The China Station: War and Diplomacy, 1830–1860* (Oxford: Clarendon Press, 1978), 316–318. For an account of operations at Fatshan Creek, see Sir William Kennedy, *Hurrah for the Life of a Sailor! Fifty Years in the Royal Navy* (Edinburgh: William Blackwood, 1900), ch. 8.

13 Graham, *China Station*, 346–352.

14 Ibid., ch. 14.

15 Quoted in Major-General G. L. Verney, *The Devil's Wind: The Story of the Naval Brigade at Lucknow* (London: Hutchinson, 1956), 76–77.

16 Ibid., 77, 130.

17 Ibid., 159.

18 Antony Wild, *The East India Company: Trade and Conquest from 1600* (London: Harper Collins, 1999), 180.

19 Frank Knight, *The Clipper Ship* (London: William Collins & Sons, 1973), ch. 6.

Further reading

Mildred Archer, *The India Office Collection of Paintings and Sculpture* (London: British Library, 1986)

C. A. Bayly, *Indian Society and the Making of the British Empire* (Cambridge: Cambridge University Press, 1990)

Robert Bickers (ed.), *Ritual and Diplomacy: The Macartney Mission to China, 1792–1794* (London: British Association for Chinese Studies, 1993)

H. V. Bowen, *Revenue and Reform: The Indian Problem in British Politics, 1757–1773* (Cambridge: Cambridge University Press, 1991)
——— , *The Business of Empire: The East India Company and Imperial Britain, 1756–1833* (Cambridge: Cambridge University Press, 2005)

H. V. Bowen, Margarette Lincoln and Nigel Rigby (eds), *The Worlds of the East India Company* (Woodbridge: Boydell, 2001)

C. R. Boxer, 'The Third Anglo-Dutch War in the East', *Mariner's Mirror*, 16 (1930), 343–86

Jaap R. Bruijn and Femme S. Gaastra (eds), *Ships, Sailors and Spices: East India Companies and their Shipping in the 16th, 17th and 18th Centuries* (Amsterdam: NEHA, 1993)

Hsin-pao Chang, *Commissioner Lin and the Opium War* (Cambridge, MA: Harvard University Press, 1964)

K. N. Chaudhuri, *The English East India Company. The Study of an Early Joint-Stock Company, 1600–1640* (London: Frank Cass, 1965)
——— , *The Trading World of Asia and the English East India Company, 1660–1760* (Cambridge: Cambridge University Press, 1978)

Evan Cotton with Charles Fawcett, *East Indiamen: The East India Company's Maritime Service* (London: The Batchwood Press, 1949)

J. L. Cranmer-Byng (ed.), *An Embassy to China: Lord Macartney's Journal, 1793–1794* (London: Longmans, 1962)

E. H. Cree, *The Cree Journals: The Voyages of Edward H. Cree, Surgeon R.N., as Related in his Private Journals, 1837–1856*, ed. Michael Levien (Exeter: Webb & Bower, 1981)

Frederick Danvers and William Foster (eds), *Letters Received by the East India Company from its Servants in the East*, 6 vols (London: Sampson Low, Marston and Co., 1896–1902)

William Foster, *The East India House: Its History and Associations* (London: John Lane, 1924)
——— , *John Company* (London: The Bodley Head, 1926)
——— , *England's Quest of Eastern Trade* (London: A. & C. Black, 1933)
——— (ed.), *The Embassy of Sir Thomas Roe to the Court of the Great Mogul, 1615–1619*, 2 vols (London: The Hakluyt Society, 1899)

Holden Furber, *Rival Empires of Trade in the Orient, 1600–1800* (Minneapolis: University of Minnesota Press, 1976)

Gerald S. Graham, *The China Station: War and Diplomacy, 1830–1860* (Oxford: Clarendon Press, 1978)

Anna Jackson and Amin Jaffer (eds), *Encounters: The Meeting of Asia and Europe, 1500–1800* (London: V&A Publications, 2004)

Denis Judd, *The Lion and the Tiger: The Rise and Fall of the British Raj, 1600–1947* (Oxford: Oxford University Press, 2005)

John Keay, *The Honourable Company: A History of the English East India Company* (London: Harper Collins, 1993)

Frank Knight, *The Clipper Ship* (London: William Collins & Sons, 1973)

Philip Lawson, *The East India Company: A History, 1600–1857* (London: Longmans, 1993)

Charles Rathbone Low, *History of the Indian Navy (1613–1863)*, 2 vols (London: Richard Bentley and Son, 1877)

Basil Lubbock (ed.), *Barlow's Journal of his Life at Sea in King's Ships, East & West Indiamen & other Merchantmen from 1659 to 1703*, 2 vols (London: Hurst & Blackett, 1934)

Kenneth Macpherson, *The Indian Ocean: A History of People and the Sea* (Oxford: Oxford University Press, 1993)

Clements R. Markham (ed.), *The Voyages of Sir James Lancaster, Kt., to the East Indies, with Abstracts of Journals of Voyages to the East Indies during the Seventeenth Century, Preserved in the India Office* (London: The Hakluyt Society, 1877)

P. J. Marshall, *East Indian Fortunes: The British in Bengal in the Eighteenth Century* (Oxford: Clarendon Press, 1976)
——— , *Bengal, the British Bridgehead: Eastern India, 1740–1828* (Cambridge: Cambridge University Press, 1987)

P. J. Marshall and Glyndwr Williams, *The Great Map of Mankind: British Perceptions of the World in the Age of Enlightenment* (Cambridge, MA: Harvard University Press, 1982)

H. B. Morse, *Chronicles of the East India Company Trading to China, 1635–1834*, 5 vols (Oxford: Clarendon Press, 1926)

C. Northcote Parkinson, *Trade in the Eastern Seas, 1793–1813* (Cambridge: Cambridge University Press, 1937)
——— , *War in the Eastern Seas, 1793–1815* (London: George Allen & Unwin, 1954)

Michael Pearson, *The Indian Ocean* (London: Routledge, 2003)

Nick Robins, *The Corporation that Changed the World* (London: Pluto Press, 2006)

Lucy Sutherland, *The East India Company in Eighteenth-Century Politics* (Oxford: Clarendon Press, 1952)

Jean Sutton, *Lords of the East: The East India Company and its Ships, 1600–1874* (London: Conway Maritime Press, 2000)

Stephen Taylor, *Storm and Conquest: The Battle for the Indian Ocean, 1809* (London: Faber and Faber, 2007)

Paul Van Dyke, *The Canton Trade: Life and Enterprise on the China Coast, 1700–1845* (Hong Kong: Hong Kong University Press, 2007)

G. L. Verney, *The Devil's Wind: The Story of the Naval Brigade at Lucknow* (London: Hutchinson, 1956)

Antony Wild, *The East India Company: Trade and Conquest from 1600* (London: Harper Collins, 1998)

J. Y. Wong, *Deadly Dreams: Opium, Imperialism and the Arrow War (1856–1860) in China* (Cambridge: Cambridge University Press, 1998)

Index